Martin MacDermott

The New Spirit of the Nation

Martin MacDermott

The New Spirit of the Nation

ISBN/EAN: 9783744797443

Printed in Europe, USA, Canada, Australia, Japan

Cover: Foto ©Thomas Meinert / pixelio.de

More available books at **www.hansebooks.com**

THE

NEW SPIRIT OF THE NATION:

OR,

BALLADS AND SONGS BY THE WRITERS OF "THE NATION."

CONTAINING SONGS AND BALLADS PUBLISHED SINCE 1845.

EDITED, WITH AN INTRODUCTION,

BY

MARTIN MacDERMOTT.

London
T. FISHER UNWIN
PATERNOSTER SQUARE

Dublin
SEALY, BRYERS & WALKER
MIDDLE ABBEY STREET

New York
P. J. KENEDY
BARCLAY STREET

MDCCCXCIV

THE

New Spirit of the Nation.

INTRODUCTION.

S O many years have gone over—a full half century—since the first edition of "The Spirit of the Nation" was published, that it may well be asked, how a "New Spirit" can be evolved now,— from what source it can be drawn, and why in any case such a collection should be published at the present time? Answers to all such enquiries the editor will endeavour to supply in the following Introduction.

The *Nation* newspaper, which was the fountain and origin of "The Spirit of the Nation," made its first appearance in the world on the 15th of October, 1842. The original poems appearing in its pages, which from the first arrested attention by reason of their striking literary merit, had won such favour and aroused such enthusiasm—political as well as poetical—that it was deemed advisable to issue in book form a collection of

them, which accordingly came out so early as May, 1843.
The little book met with an immediate and an immense
success ; and it continued to appear in successive editions
(and additions) until the 1st of January, 1845, when it
arrived at its maturity in the form of a handsome quarto
volume ; many of the songs being set to ancient or
original music, and the whole enclosed in a very beautiful
cover, designed by a notable Irish artist,—whose name
I am not at liberty to disclose.

This is the " Spirit of the Nation," as it has been
known from that day to this—the *vade mecum* of Irish
patriotism—which has gone the round of the world;
whose kindling thoughts and musical words have been
a cherished possession in Irish homes,—not only within
the four seas of Ireland, but on every distant shore to
which inexorable fate has driven her exiles. Still, taken
as representing the whole volume of song produced by
the writers of the *Nation*, it is clearly inadequate. In the
first place the verses it contains do not go beyond the end
of the year 1845, although, for many years after that date,
the stream of poetry continued to flow plenteously from
the fountain-head. If it be asked why there was so
sudden a cessation in the work of collection, the answer
is not far to seek. It is, that in the autumn of that year,
1845, an event occurred which so overwhelmed the editor
of the *Nation*,—at first with grief, and afterwards with
new cares and duties,—that he had no longer leisure left
for devoting himself to the task of completing the collection.
That event was the death of Thomas Davis ; in fact, the
history of the *Nation* newspaper may be divided into
three well-defined periods—of which the one terminating
with Davis's death is the first ; the next extending to the
catastrophe of '48, when the presses of the *Nation* were
broken up by order of the English government; and the
last between '49 and '55, at which latter date the founder
and editor of the great Irish journal closed his stormy and
illustrious editorial career, and bade adieu to Ireland.

Now, only the verses belonging to the first of these three
periods having found a place in " The Spirit of the
Nation," as hitherto published, it has been thought well

—while there still remain some relics of our ancient confederacy of song,—while, above all, its founder is still amongst us with guidance and enthusiasm, as in the old days,—to gather together into a " NEW SPIRIT OF THE NATION," not only so much of the old as may still be considered in the land of the living, but also the most popular part of the poetical literature produced by the *Nation* in the second and third periods to which I have referred.   In this way, it is hoped, something like an adequate representation may be bequeathed to future generations of the part taken by "Young Ireland" in the great work, still to be completed, of building up a National Literature.   Fully to carry out this purpose, two volumes will be required ; of which this, the first, is devoted to the poetry published in the *Nation* after the death of Davis.   In due course a second volume will be issued, should the favour of readers warrant it, containing all the more popular poems which have appeared in the old "Spirit of the Nation," along with others, from the same source originally, but which have found their way into publications to which they do not so rightfully belong.*   When this purpose has been fully achieved, and something like a complete collection made of the best of the poetical contributions from writers of the *Nation* to the national stock, it will be found, I think, that Young Ireland, as a political party—of which the *Nation* newspaper was the accredited representative—has furnished a larger quota of literary effort, especially in the region of song, and has wielded a wider and deeper influence in that way—contemporaneously and subsequently—than any other political organization which our country has seen.   Is this claiming too much ?   Let the reader recall what the last century has left us in this kind of poetical literature.   The days of

---

* *E.g.* MacCarthy's "Book of Irish Ballads,"—Edward Hayes's " Ballads of Ireland,"—Connolly's " Household Library of Ireland" (New York); with a host of other compilations— English, Irish, Scotch, American and Australian, down to the present day.

Grattan, with so splendid a record for eloquence and patriotism, had not many poets to sing them ; a few songs, and these not of the first order, are all that survive.* Of the men of '98 also it may be said that their courage and patriotism were great, but their lyrists far from numerous. After the Union came Moore ; but Moore's "*Melodies*" have been well described by Duffy as "the wail of a lost cause." The poet has relinquished in them the very accent of freedom, besides being, so far as words and style go, more English than the English themselves. For these reasons, and others which cannot be discussed here, Moore never did, and never could, reach the heart of the Gaelic people.† Neither was the long tribunate of O'Connell prolific in poetry. He himself, except un- consciously, was no poet. During his thirty years of splendid labour for Ireland, it is true, he stirred the nation to its depths. He drove his oratorical plough- share deep into the national soil in every direction, turning it over, furrowing it—but *sowing no seeds*. It was reserved for the Young Irelanders—the men of ideas, the men of convictions, the men of purpose— to sow broadcast in fields that had long lain fallow. They were the sowers who found the good ground, which has brought forth fruit to them some thirty, some sixty, some a hundred fold.

Of the influence exerted over the Irish people by the

* Drennan's and Curran's chiefly.

† Moore, however, by his songs, conferred one inestimable service on Ireland, by breaking through the barrier of prejudice and distrust which had divided the two nations. As there are missionary priests who have to acquire the language of the people to whom the truth is to be preached, so there are missi- onary poets and orators. Moore was a missionary poet ; Burke (so far as his labours for Ireland extended), a missionary orator. But what the almost inspired eloquence and wisdom of Burke failed to accomplish, Moore—with his bright wit, charming poetry and enchanting music—easily effected. His instrument was not the harp, whose strings he is so fond of invoking, but the piano of the great Whig *salons*. Like St. Patrick, he sang his listeners into conversion.—ED.

songs and ballads of the *Nation*, it is too late in the day now to raise a question ; the *fact* of that influence is patent, and has been acknowledged everywhere.   Davis, Duffy and the rest may have lacked some of the literary skill, finish, genius even, of Moore ; they may not have reached the standard of aesthetic super-excellence demanded by some of our young critics and poets of the present day ; but they knew their way, at least, straight into the hearts of the people, and they struck a chord there which has been vibrating ever since ;—a chord responsive, not to the poetic merits of the verses alone, but to the patriotic spirit which they breathe.   For it must be remembered that in the national creed of Young Ireland, poetry was only a means ;—the end and purpose of every ballad and song being, to rouse the nation into enthusiasm for Ireland as a Nation, and for the cause of national freedom.   There is scarcely a verse in this collection through which this purpose does not shine ; and therefore in claiming for Young Ireland a larger share of poetical inspiration than any other political movement has called forth, I should add that all the strings of the Young Ireland harp have but one burthen—and that is—*love of country*.

As to the reception these verses met with on their first appearance from writers of repute in literary criticism, have we not read the unstinted praise which Lord Jeffrey gave to the " Ballad Poetry of Ireland," and especially to Mangan ; and how Macaulay—while deploring, of course, their tendency, was much struck with the energy and beauty of some of the songs in the " Spirit of the Nation ;" how Miss Mitford became enthusiastic over Davis's ballads ; and how even the *Times* awarded to the literary excellence of Duffy's great ballad—" The Muster of the North," what its author is fain to consider " extravagant praise."*   Nor ought one to omit, in this appreciation, the close attention which the law officers of the Crown in Ireland bestowed (not gratuitously I am afraid) on the literary

---

* Richard Lalor Shiel considered " The Muster of the North " equal to any piece of ballad-poetry he had ever read.

labours of Young Ireland. In one of the prefaces to the old "Spirit of the Nation," the writer makes the Solicitor-General not only recite some of poems in court, but express his regret that he was not able to sing one of them—" The Memory of the Dead "—to the jury ! This, of course, may be a playful exaggeration ; but there is no doubt of the pains these learned gentlemen took in following, from week to week, the poetical literature of the *Nation;* nor is it without amusement that one sees—in the copy of that journal preserved at the British Museum, the identical lines referred to above, duly initialled by the Crown-Solicitor, as an exhibit.°

One beneficent change, which Davis and the leaders of Young Ireland were the means of bringing about by their writings, was so important and so far-reaching in its effects, that I think it ought not to be passed over, even in such a cursory review as the present. Although Dublin, like Edinburgh, has never been without refined and cultured literary society, made up mainly of its professional and academic citizens, there has been no period, perhaps, in its history—at least during the present century—when it stood so high in this respect as during the Forties. I have no space here to do much more than enumerate names ; but any one familiar with the time will recognise, in each name, a celebrity in some department of intellectual activity. There was George Petrie—great antiquary, delightful artist, enthusiastic and most learned musician—a host in himself ; there were the world-famed physicians, Graves and Stokes, as eminent for their personal worth as for their distinguished ability ; there were Dr. Todd and the other Dons of Trinity College : there was John O'Donovan, greatest of Gaelic scholars ; there was Samuel Ferguson, who, besides possessing many other high qualifications, was unquestionably the greatest Irish poet of his generation ; there were even one or two stray lords ; and there were a number of other able men whose names I am unable to find room for. Now, all these

* In *Reg. v. O'Connell,* and others, 1844.

were good Irishmen, after their fashion, and devoted students of, and believers in, Ireland's greatness in the past ;
but very few of them, I believe, if any, had any leaning
towards the idea of a nationality for the present time,
until the advent of the *Nation.* After that, I think, there
was a great change. I will not assert that everyone of
these distinguished men was won over completely to the
national idea, though some of the most eminent were—
Petrie,* Ferguson, Stokes, O'Donovan, certainly—and all
were leavened with the more generous spirit of the new
teaching. Considering the intellectual calibre of these
men, and the influence that spread from each of them
as a centre, I believe that the *Nation* never did a greater
service to Ireland than in leading them away from the
narrow circle of intolerance in which they had been bred.
Nor must it be forgotten that three, at least, of the
eminent men I have mentioned as illustrating the last
generation of Irishmen have, or have had, their repre-
sentatives in this—equally distinguished, and, I believe,
equally patriotic.

As to the enduring pepularity of the "Spirit of the
Nation," I need only cite two witnesses, both of them
possessed of the widest experience of the popular feeling—
the late Justice O'Hagan and William O'Brien, M.P. The
former, who may indeed be regarded as no inconsider-
able a contributor to the success he records, writes:†—

* In a letter written by Petrie to his friend, Lord Adare,
there is the following passage showing at least how habitually he
turned for solace to the pages of the *Nation.* It was written on
the day after signing the last proof of his monumental work on
the Round Towers. "Yesterday was a memorable day in my
life, and yet I never felt more calm and reconciled than I did
during the whole of it. About five o'clock the turmoil was over,
no proofs coming in, or to come, the house empty of scribes and
tranquil ; dined and sat down *to read the Nation* at the drawing-
room fire with my glass of punch beside me."—Stokes' "Life of
Petrie."

† In an article contributed to the *Freeman's Journal* on Sir
Charles Gavan Duffy's "Young Ireland."

"When he" (Mr. Cowan, then member for Newcastle) "said that '48 had been not a failure, but a success, he spoke a truth of which ample evidence exists in the fact that the prose and poetry, the names and history, of that time *are known and cherished by the people of Ireland to the exclusion of all other literature and history.*" And the latter :* "As surely as you will find in the heart of every Irish maiden a love message, so surely, deep down in the heart of every young Irishman, you will find the ' Spirit of the Nation.'" Remember too that this opinion was recorded forty-five years after the first appearance of the book to which it refers.

Perhaps, however, no better proof can be had of the vitality of any literary work, be it ballad or book, than the continued call for its republication, decade after decade. Judged by this test, what volume published within the last fifty years comes out better than our dear old "Spirit of the Nation"? Not only have its green leaves appeared every year as regularly as those of Spring,—but they have out-rivalled the record of those unfailing visitors. For, this very year (1893) being the jubilee year of the book, its editions, I believe, already number some fifty-four ; while the copies circulating in the greater Ireland beyond the Atlantic and Pacific, far exceed even this total.

Such being the state of the case, does it not behove us, I would ask, to requite this singular amount of public favour by making the book, if we can, even worthier of acceptance at the hands of the readers of the present generation ?—an object which, it is considered, cannot be better attained than by gathering together in the same volume all that the old "Spirit of the Nation" holds of a permanent value ; while enriching it with the verses, hitherto uncollected, which are known to have received the stamp of national approval. Which, briefly, I may be allowed to repeat, is the aim and purpose of "THE NEW SPIRIT OF THE NATION."

* In his novel, "When we were Boys."

And now, let me add a few words concerning the writers, or some of them, to whom the following pages owe their value.

Omitting for the present the names belonging to the former " Spirit "—nearly all of which I think reappear here ; the first on our muster-roll, the laureate of the later contingent as Davis was of the earlier, is Thomas D'Arcy McGee. McGee was born in 1825, and had not yet reached his twentieth year when he returned from his first visit to America, just before Davis's death, to accept an appointment on the staff of the *Freeman's Journal*, from which, however, he speedily passed to the *Nation*. But young as he was, he had already become known as speaker, lecturer, and newspaper-writer in the United States. In fact, some of his earliest utterances there received contemporary praise from so excellent a judge as O'Connell; just as his last speech, spoken on the very night he was murdered, won unqualified commendation from Mr. Gladstone. McGee had been an early contributor to the poetry of the *Nation*. A ballad of his, " The Battle of Leitrim," which appeared early in 1843, seems to me to have caught already the antique Ossianic spirit which distinguishes, in so marked a degree, many of his later poems.* As a rule, however, his early contributions are far from being his best. His name does not figure at all amongst the contributors to " The Spirit of the Nation." It was only after 1848, and when he had left Ireland for ever, that McGee found the full measure of his power as a poet. Perhaps the most striking fact in connection with the story of McGee's poetry is this,—that the more his exile was prolonged, the more intensely Irish became his verse.† Even the change which unhappily came over his

* *E.g.* :—"Their giant forms shone in the flood
    Like mighty spirits long departed ;
    For they were strong, and warm of blood,
    Swift as the elk, and lion-hearted ! "

† It should be mentioned that some of the poems by Thomas D'Arcy McGee in this collection were originally published in the *New York Nation*. This was merely the *Nation* under another form.

political opinions during his later years appears not to
have abated, but rather increased, his love for what was
native and Irish.   At the time when his voice was loud in
the parliament of his adopted country in favour of Im-
perialism, when his pen, in the " History of Ireland," could
find excuses for Pitt, and scarce an execration even for
Castlereagh ; the poet still yearned with love and longing
towards the distant island of his birth.   To use his own
words :—" Its hills still surrounded his heart like a wall,
and its paths were all winding through his brain."   The
glory of Keltic Erin, the ancient skill of her builders, the
piety of her saints, the erudition of her priests, the zeal
and patience of the old " Four Masters," all these form
subjects for sympathetic record, in words laden with the
gravity and sweetness of the Past.   It is this archaic note
which he has caught as truly, I think, even as Ferguson
and more so than Clarence Mangan, which distinguishes
him among the poets of Young Ireland.   One ought not
to forget, either, that as one great Irishman after another
was laid in his grave—John O'Donovan, Eugene O'Curry,
Richard D'Alton Williams, William Smith O'Brien—it was
McGee who gave a voice to their country's lamentation in
verses worthy of their fame.   How pathetic, too, are some
of his own personal questionings and avowals :—" Am I
remembered in Erin ? "   " The land I adore."

> " I'd rather turn one simple verse
>   True to the Gaelic ear,
> Than Sapphic odes I might rehearse
>   With senates listening near."

Such faithful evidence of McGee's persistent love of
country will be surely remembered long after his political
aberrations are forgotten ; while the sudden and tragic
close of a career, so freighted with labour and so illustrious,
must ever arouse the abhorrence and the pity of every
right thinking Irishman.   •
McGee's countenance was not pleasing, from its de-

cided African cast and woolly hair, characteristics as strongly marked in him as in the Alexandre Dumas, *père et fils.* This negro race-mark, in Irishmen, I have noticed in two or three other instances; and I can only attribute it to a probable descent from one of those faithful countrymen of ours whom Cromwell and his son Henry sent as slaves to the West Indies, and who may be presumed to have married women of African blood. Though McGee's face was somewhat heavy and unpleasing in repose, it lit up wonderfully under excitement; and as he was tall, of a fine presence, and perfect in voice and delivery, his oratory was most impressive. Taking him all round, McGee was far and away the finest speaker of the party— superior even to Meagher, who required time and labour for his addresses—whereas McGee's gift was spontaneous and always at his command. He was murdered at Ottawa, about midnight, on April 7th, 1868, having been shot through the head, from behind, as he was leaning down to put the latch-key in the door of his lodgings. He was murdered by a miscreant of his own nation.

Clarence Mangan—I give him the name by which he is best known, although his baptismal name was James and " Clarence " assumed—belongs to an earlier period than most of the other writers in the *Nation.* Duffy, who reverenced Mangan's genius and had known the man and loved him in spite of his failings years before the *Nation* came to be founded, naturally sought the assistance of his brilliant pen for the new journal. Accordingly the poetical address to its readers which ushered in the first number was from him. It has all his dash, brilliancy, marvellous power of diction, and easy flow of numbers; but it is little more than an *annonce*, and contains much more chaff than solid grain. It was Duffy himself in his " Fagh a Beallach " who struck the first serious note of the new minstrelsy in the third number of the paper, to be followed after a brief interval by Davis's " Lament for Owen Roe " and O'Hagan's " Ourselves Alone." Beyond " The *Nation's* First Number " there occurs only one piece by Mangan which is not written in the same light spirit of raillery until after Davis's death.* Nor was it until 1846 that Mangan put forth all his power in the great sweeping odes which he calls "The Warning Voice" and "The Peal of Another Trumpet." In these he appears almost more of a prophet than a poet. In fact, Mangan seems to have realised more than any of the poets of that day the dark significance of the crisis then impending over the country. Famine, Fever, Pestilence, and Death cast their shadows over his verse, endowing it with a dread solemnity. Perhaps he may have felt a foreboding that he himself was doomed to go down in the general cataclysm.

Another class of subjects which Mangan largely contributed to the *Nation* at this time—specimens of which may be found in this collection—are translations from the Irish—generally of the 16th or 17th centuries, but sometimes of a remoter date, like that wonderful rendering of *The Hymn of St. Patrick*, in which, contrary to his wont, he has reproduced almost word for word the ancient text, but with such a mastery of rhyme and rhythm that the new work appears as perfect as the old. It is said of Mangan that he did not understand the ancient language, and that these translations—fine and spirited and faithful as some

* It was in Petrie's *Dublin Penny Journal* (1832-3) and *Irish Penny Journal* (1840) that Mangan published, under the pseudonym of "Clarence," most of the pieces which made his early reputation. The "New Year's Night of a Miserable Man," a noble poetical rendering of Jean Paul's prose, and "The One Mystery" (original) appeared in the former of these publications. The great "Lament for the Tyrone Princes," "The Woman of Three Cows," "Kincora," in the latter. Petrie, O'Donovan, Curry, Aubrey de Vere (the elder), Carleton, Ferguson, Anster—all contributed to these volumes, which Southey considered amongst the most valuable in his library. The illustrations (devoted exclusively to Irish subjects) are also of great merit. No. 14 of the *I. P. J.* contains a sketch of "Paddy Coneely," the blind Galway piper, by Frederick Burton, with a notice of him by Petrie, both inimitably well done. Gleanings from these journals would form an admirable book.

of them are—were made from word for word renderings supplied to him by such Gaelic scholars as O'Donovan, O'Curry, or his friend Daly, the printer, of Anglesey Street. Yet it is hard to believe that, scholar and linguist as Mangan was, he could have passed ten years of his life in daily and intimate social intercourse with such masters of Irish learning as O'Donovan, O'Curry, and Wakeman* without picking up *(malgré lui)* a sufficient knowledge of a language not very difficult to acquire. Be this as it may, however acquired, his translations from the Irish have a weird and unmodern stamp peculiarly their own. . . . All students of Irish literature have been made familiar with the sad life-history of Mangan. What he might have accomplished had he been other than he was it seems a vain thing to inquire. The wonder must always be— given the facts of his life—that he has been able to leave to us so much beautiful work, for the facts of his life are tragic beyond all written tragedy. The contrast between a splendid and cultivated genius and a life spent in utter squalidness and misery must always be terrible ; and this contrast, heightened and rendered more pitiful by his periodical indulgence in excesses, is furnished by at least a part of our poor Mangan's life. The wonderful thing is that in spite of everything he retained to the last not only his splendid play of fancy, not only the marvellous power which he possessed over his thoughts and language, but also a singular piety, simplicity, and purity of feeling. The finest of his poems were contributed to the *Nation* at a time when he and his brother (co-partners in misery though not in genius) were spending their time in migrations from one wretched garret to another, with scarce a rush-light to read by at night, a bed to lie on, or a blanket to cover them.† Not that Mangan was without friends ever ready

---

* In the office of the Archæological Department of the Ordnance Survey of Ireland.

† This statement, which is made on the authority of Father Meehan, is perhaps too general in its terms. It may have referred only to the last year or two of Mangan's life. Sir Gavan

to lend him a helping hand, but of what avail was this to a man who spent all he got in drink? This vice, however, was really the only one to which he was addicted. When released from his besettiug sin, as sometimes for long intervals he was wont to be, there was no more gentle, compassionate, tender, or pious soul than Clarence Mangan. He was forty-six when the end came to him, in one of the wards of the Meath Hospital in Dublin, of the after effects of an attack of cholera—the famine epidemic.*
. . . Once only I met him, and then but for a few minutes. He appeared to me just as he is described by Mitchel and Father Meehan, except that one peculiarity which struck me greatly appears to have escaped their notice—the intense blue of his eyes, which were of a deep ultra-marine, like the waters of Lake Leman. I have only seen in one other countenance eyes of the same brilliancy and depth of colour. The effect was startling in a face otherwise so wan.

A new and distinctive feature of the *Nation* minstrelsy after 1845 was the presence for the first time of a band of women poets. The first to lead this choir was young Ellen Downing, the Cork girl known as "Mary of the Nation." Only 17 when her first contribution appeared †
(which, sooth to say, did not give very much promise), it was only a little after Davis's death that her real power became apparent. Ellen Downing's poetical existence—at least politically—lasted but three years in all, yet some of her verses will always be sure of a place in every collection of Irish song. They possess a simple charm—of directness, of candour—which is indescribably winning and entirely their own. One notices, too, a vein of strong sense running through them, like a vein of iron, which,

---

Duffy considers it as being greatly exaggerated. He says :—" I have visited Mangan in his lodgings, which were poor, but not squalid. I never saw him affected by drink. Opium was supposed to be his temptation."
* On the 20th of June, 1849.
† In May, 1845.

combined with their tenderness and humour, is essentially the mark of an Irishwoman.*

" Mary " was a Munster girl—one of our own—a child of the clans as it were ; but the next poetess whose voice was raised on our side came from what might be called the enemy's camp. A young lady of fashion, daughter of a dignitary of the Irish Church—Miss Jane Francesca Elgee—could scarcely have been taught to regard with sympathy the native poor people whom she saw suffering around her, or the men who had embraced their cause. But, in the end, no voice that was raised in the cause of the poor and the oppressed, none that denounced political wrong-doing in Ireland, was more eagerly listened to than that of the graceful and accomplished woman known in literature as " Speranza " and in society as Lady Wilde.

When the presses of the *Nation* were broken up by the Government in 1848 the last article that came from their type and the most defiant—" Jacta Alea Est "—was from the pen of " Speranza." Her poems are characterized by a certain epic or scriptural largeness of utterance—a sweeping and overmastering melody and a strain of majestic thought. Womanlike, she has a heart " open as day to melting charity." The sights and scenes of the famine year appear to have gone through her with the sharpness of a sword. But, in speaking of them, her tone is so high that one is reminded of what Fuseli said of Michael Angelo—" A beggar rose from his hands *the patriarch of poverty.*"†

---

* Ellen Downing was also a most charming correspondent. A number of her letters, addressed to the editor of the *Nation*, have been placed in the hands of the present editor for publication. Along with her poems I think they would form a most attractive volume, which, I hope, may be deemed worthy of a place in the new " Irish Library."

† As an illustration of Speranza's *grand manner*, the follow

There were other fair Irish girls who sang, and sang well—as may be seen from examples given in this volume —in the *Nation* choir, but none, I think, with the sway and penetrating influence of these two.

Another name, it occurs to me, ought not to be forgotten here—that of William James Linton—the eager English Chartist of those days, the admirable artist and engraver, who, under the pseudonym of "Spartacus," enriched the pages of the *Nation* with many very striking poems. His name deserves not to be omitted, because he elected to fight as a brother in our ranks at a time when English sympathy for Irish wrongs was far rarer than it is now His poetical pieces, which are very numerous, formed a kind of miniature epic embracing in its cycle nearly every aspect of the Irish trouble, each poem dealing with some one particular phase of it—landlord tyranny, the tenant's revenge, famine, eviction, emigration, exile—each of these forming the subject of one or many lyrics—closing with the prophetic victory of right over wrong, and with a beautiful picture of Ireland as she shall be when happiness and comfort are restored :—

> The Happy Land !
> Studded with cheerful homesteads fair to see
> With garden grace and household symmetry—
> How grand the wide-browed peasant's lordly mien,
> The matron's smile serene—
> O happy, happy land!

Of these excellent poems only very few can be given in this collection ; but, with the title :—" Ireland for the Irish : Rhymes and Reasons against Landlordism " :— they have been published in New York, where Mr. Linton has long resided, and they are still well worth reading.

ing, which occurs in some lines on the death of O'Connell, reads like a translation from Dante :—

> " Seeking the gates of God's great Church on earth,
> He found the gates of Heaven, and entered in."

Here, then, the editor may pause.   He hopes to have a few further words to address to the reader when Part II. is called for.

MARTIN MacDERMOTT.

THE NEW SPIRIT OF THE NATION.

LIST OF POEMS.

NEW SPIRIT OF THE NATION.

THE KELTS

LONG, long ago, beyond the misty space
  Of twice a thousand years,
In Erin old there dwelt a mighty race
  Taller than Roman spears;
Like oaks and towers, they had a giant grace,
  Were fleet as deers:
With winds and waves they made their biding place,
  The ·Western shepherd seers.

Their ocean-god was *Manaman Mac Lir,*
  Whose angry lips
In their white foam full often would inter
  Whole fleets of ships:
Crom was their day-god, and their thunderer
  Made morning and eclipse:
Bride was their queen of song, and unto her
  They pray'd with fire-touch'd lips.

Great were their acts, their passions, and their sports ;
    With clay and stone
They piled on strath and shore those mystic forts,
    Not yet undone ;
On cairn-crown'd hills they held their council courts ;
    While youths—alone—
With giant-dogs, explored the elks' resorts,
    And brought them down.

Of these was *Finn*, the father of the bard
    Whose ancient song
Over the clamour of all change is heard,
    Sweet-voiced and strong.
Finn once o'ertook Granu, the golden hair'd,
    The fleet and young :
From her, the lovely, and from him, the feared,
    The primal poet sprung—

Ossian !—two thousand years of mist and change
    Surround thy name ;
Thy Finnian heroes now no longer range
    The hills of Fame.
The very name of Finn and Gael sound strange ;
    Yet thine the same
By miscall'd lake and desecrated grange
    Remains, and shall remain !

The Druid's altar and the Druid's creed
    We scarce can trace ;

There is not left an undisputed deed
  Of all your race—
Save your majestic Song, which hath their speed,
  And strength, and grace:
In that sole song they live, and love, and bleed—
  It bears them on through space.

Inspirèd giant, shall we e'er behold,
  In our own time,
One fit to speak your spirit on the wold,
  Or seize your rhyme?
One pupil of the past, as mighty-soul'd
  As in the prime
Were the fond, fair, and beautiful, and bold—
  They of your song sublime?

Thomas D'Arcy McGee.

ARGAN MÓR.

AIR.—*Argan Mor.*

THE Danes rush around, around ;
To the edge of the fosse they bound ;
Hark ! hark, to their trumpets' sound,
      Bidding them to the war.
Hark ! hark to their cruel cry,
As they swear our hearts' cores to dry,
And their Raven red to dye ;
      Glutting their demon, Thor.

Leaping the Rath upon,
Here's the fiery Ceallachàn—
He makes the Lochlonnach* wan,
      Lifting his brazen spear !
Ivor, the Dane, is struck down,
For the spear broke right through his crown ;
Yet worse did the battle frown—
      Anlaf is on our rere !

See ! see ! the Rath's gates are broke !
And in—in, like a cloud of smoke,
Burst on the dark Danish folk,
      Charging us everywhere—
Oh, never was closer fight
Than in Argan Mór that night—
How little do men want light,
      Fighting within their lair.

* Northmen,

Then girding about our king,
On the thick of the foes we spring—
Down—down we trample and fling,
    Gallantly though they strive :
And never our falchions stood,
Till we were all wet with their blood,
And none of the pirate brood
    Went from the Rath alive !

THOMAS DAVIS.

THE ANCIENT RACE.

[This poem was written at the era of the Irish Tenant League
(from 1850-56), when the principles of the land struggle were
first defined and formulated.]

WHAT shall become of the ancient race,
The noble Keltic island race?
Like cloud on cloud o'er the azure sky,
When winter storms are loud and high,
Their dark ships shadow the ocean's face—
What shall become of the Keltic race?

What shall befal the ancient race—
The poor, unfriended, faithful race?
Where ploughman's song made the hamlet ring,
The hawk and the owlet flap their wing ;
The village homes, oh, who can trace—
God of our persecuted race !

What shall befal the ancient race?
Is treason's stigma on their face?
Be they cowards or traitors? Go--
Ask the shade of England's foe;
See the gems her crown that grace;
They tell a tale of the ancient race.

They tell a tale of the ancient race—
Of matchless deeds in danger's face;
They speak of Britain's glory fed
·With blood of Kelts, right bravely shed;
Of India's spoil and Frank's disgrace—
Such tale they tell of the ancient race.

Then why cast out the ancient race?
Grim want dwelt with the ancient race,
And hell-born laws, with prison jaws;
And greedy lords, with tiger maws,
Have swallowed—swallow still apace—
The limbs and blood of the ancient race.

Will no one shield the ancient race?
They fly their fathers' burial-place;
The proud lords with the heavy purse,
Their fathers' shame—their people's curse—
Demons in heart, nobles in face—
They dig a grave for the ancient race!

What shall befal the ancient race.
Shall all forsake their dear birth-place,
Without one struggle strong to keep
The old soil where their fathers sleep?
The dearest land on earth's wide space—
Why leave it so, O, ancient race?

What shall befal the ancient race?
Light up one hope for the ancient race;
Oh, priest of God—Soggarth Aroon!
Lead but the way, we'll go full soon;
Is there a danger we will not face,
To keep old homes for the Irish race?

They shall not go, the ancient race—
They must not go, the ancient race!
Come, gallant Kelts, and take your stand—
And form a league to save the land;
The land of faith, the land of grace,
The land of Erin's ancient race!

They must not go, the ancient race!
They shall not go, the ancient race!
The cry swells loud from shore to shore,
From emerald vale to mountain hoar,
From altar high to market-place—
"THEY SHALL NOT GO, the ancient race!"

(REVD.) J. F. TORMY.

C

GLENGARIFF.

AIR—O'Sullivan's March.

I WANDERED at eve by Glengariff's sweet water,
  Half in the shade, and half in the moon,
And thought of the time when the Sacsanach slaughter
  Reddened the night and darkened the noon ;
Mo nuar ! mo nuar ! mo nuar ! * I said—
    When I think, in this valley and sky—
    Where true lovers and poets should sigh—
Of the time when its chieftain O'Sullivan fled.

Then my mind went along with O'Sullivan marching
  Over Musk'ry's moors and Ormond's plain,
His *curachs* the waves of the Shannon o'erarching,
  And his pathway mile-marked with the slain ;
Mo nuar! mo nuar! mo nuar! I said—
    Yet 'twas better far from you to go,
    And to battle with torrent and foe,
Than linger as slaves where your sweet waters spread.

But my fancy burst on, like a clan o'er the border,
  To times that seemed almost at hand,
When grasping her banner, old Erin's *Lamh Laidir*
  Alone shall rule over the rescued land :
O baotho! O baotho! O baotho! † I said—
    Be our marching as steady and strong,
    And freemen our valleys shall throng,
When the last of our foemen is vanquished and fled !

          * Alas !   † Oh, fine.

THOMAS DAVIS.

GLENGARIFF AND ADRIGOOLE.

How soft is the moon on Glengariff!
  The rocks seem to melt with the light—
Oh, would I were there with dear Annie
  To tell her that love is as bright;
And nobly the sun of July
  O'er the waters of Adrigoole shines,
Oh, would that I saw the Green Banner
  Wave there over conquering lines!

Oh, love is more fair than the moonlight,
  And glory more grand than the sun,
And there is no rest for a brave heart
  Till its bride, and its laurels, are won;
But next to the burst of our banner,
  And the smile of dear Annie, I crave
The moon on the rocks of Glengariff—
  The sun upon Adrigoole's wave.

THOMAS DAVIS.

BRIGHT FAIRIES BY GLENGARIFF'S BAY.

AIR—*Fanny Power*.

[This song possesses, with the two which precede it, a melancholy interest, as being amongst the last written by Davis.   The
subject of the two last given was the lady to whom he was
engaged when he died.   The true name, which for obvious
reasons was suppressed in the original text is here given—Annie
not Fanny:—Miss Annie Hutton of Dublin.   The reader may
observe that only the poems of Davis which appeared after his
death are printed in this volume.—ED.]

BRIGHT fairies by Glengariff's bay,
Soft woods that o'er Killarney sway,
Bold echoes born in Céim-an-eich,
         Your kinsman's greeting hear !
He asks you, by old friendship's name,
By all the rights that minstrels claim,
For Erin's joy and Desmond's fame,
         Be kind to Annie dear !

Her eyes are darker than Dunloe,
Her soul is whiter than the snow,
Her tresses like arbutus flow,
         Her step like frighted deer :
Then, still thy waves, capricious lake !
And ceaseless, soft winds, round her wake,
Yet never bring a cloud to break
         The smile of Annie dear !

Oh ! let her see the trance-bound men,
And kiss the red deer in his den,
And spy from out a hazel glen
         O'Donoghue appear ;—

Or, should she roam by wild Dunbwy,
Oh ! send the maiden to her knee,
Whilome I sung,—but then, ah ! me,
      I knew not Annie dear !

Old Mangerton ! thine eagles plume—
Dear Innisfallen ! brighter bloom—
And Mucruss ! whisper thro' the gloom
      Quaint legends to her ear :
Till strong as ash-tree in its pride,
And gay as sunbeam on the tide,
We welcome back to Liffey's side,
      Our brightest, Annie dear.

THOMAS DAVIS.

SWEET SYBIL.

My Love is as fresh as the morning sky,
  My Love is as soft as the summer air,
My Love is as true as the saints on high,
  And never was saint so fair !
    Oh glad is my heart, when I name her name,
      For it sounds like a song to me—
    I'll love you, it sings, nor heed their blame,
      For you love me, Astór machree !

Sweet Sybil! sweet Sybil! my heart is wild
  With the fairy spell that her eyes have lit ;
I sit in a dream where my Love has smiled,
  I kiss where her name is writ!
      Oh, darling, I fly like a dreamy boy,
        The toil that is joy to the strong and true ;
      The life that the brave for their land employ
        I squander in dreams of you.

The face of my Love has the changeful light
  That gladdens the sparkling sky of spring ;
The voice of my Love is a strange delight
  As when birds in the May-time sing.
      Oh, hope of my heart ! oh, light of my life !
        Oh come to me, darling, with peace and rest !
      Oh come like the summer, my own sweet wife !
        To your home in my longing breast.

Be blessèd the home sweet Sybil will sway
  With the glance of her soft and queenly eyes ;
Oh, happy the love young Sybil will pay
  With the breath of her tender sighs !
      That home is the hope of my waking dreams—
        That love fills my eyes with pride—
      There's light in their glance, there's joy in their
        beams,
        When I think of my own young bride.

CHARLES GAVAN DUFFY.

DARK ROSALEEN.

[This fine poem is a paraphrase from a Gaelic original, entitled, "Roisin Dubh" (The Black Little Rose), in Hardiman's Collection, supposed to have been written in the reign of Elizabeth by a bard of Hugh O'Donnell *the Red*, one of the banished earls. The original is much simpler than the translation—so called—to which it appears to have supplied no more than the *motif* of each of the verses.]

O MY Dark Rosaleen,
   Do not sigh, do not weep!
The priests are on the ocean green,
   They march along the Deep.
There's wine . . . from the royal Pope,
   Upon the ocean green;
And Spanish ale shall give you hope,
   My Dark Rosaleen!
   My own Rosaleen!
Shall glad your heart, shall give you hope,
Shall give you health, and help, and hope,
   My Dark Rosaleen.

Over hills, and through dales,
   Have I roamed for your sake;
All yesterday I sailed with sails
   On river and on lake.
The Erne . . . at its highest flood,
   I dashed across unseen,
For there was lightning in my' blood
   My Dark Rosaleen!
   My own Rosaleen!

Oh ! there was lightning in my blood,
Red lightning lightened through my blood,
My Dark Rosaleen !

All day long in unrest,
To and fro do I move,
The very soul within my breast
Is wasted for you, love !
The heart . . . in my bosom faints
To think of you, my Queen,
My life of life, my saint of saints,
My Dark Rosaleen !
My own Rosaleen !
To hear your sweet and sad complaints,
My life, my love, my saint of saints,
My Dark Rosaleen !

Woe and pain, pain and woe,
Are my lot, night and noon,
To see your bright face clouded so,
Like to the mournful moon.
But yet . . . will I rear your throne
Again in golden sheen ;
'Tis you shall reign, shall reign alone,
My Dark Rosaleen !
My own Rosaleen !
'Tis you shall have the golden throne,
'Tis you shall reign, and reign alone,
My Dark Rosaleen !

Over dews, over sands,
   Will I fly, for your weal:
Your holy delicate white hands
   Shall girdle me with steel.
At home . . . in your emerald bowers,
   From morning's dawn till e'en,
You'll pray for me, my flower of flowers,
   My Dark Rosaleen !
   My fond Rosaleen !
You'll think of me through Daylight's hours,
My virgin flower, my flower of flowers,
   My dark Rosaleen !

I could scale the blue air,
   I could plough the high hills,
Oh, I could kneel all night in prayer
   To heal your many ills !
And one . . . beamy smile from you
   Would float like light between
My toils and me, my own, my true,
   My Dark Rosaleen !
   My fond Rosaleen !
Would give me life and soul anew,
A second life, a soul anew,
   My Dark Rosaleen !

Oh ! the Erne shall run red
   With redundance of blood,
The earth shall rock beneath our tread,
   And flames wrap hill and wood,

And gun-peal, and slogan cry,
　　Wake many a glen serene,
Ere you shall fade, ere you shall die,
　　My Dark Rosaleen !
　　My own Rosaleen !
The Judgment Hour must first. be nigh,
Ere you can fade, ere you can die,
　　My Dark Rosaleen !

———

EDUCATION.

["In Scotland what a work have the four-and-twenty letters to show for them elves ! The natural enemies of vice, and folly and slavery; the great sowers, but the still great weeders of the human soil."—*John Philpot Curran.*]

IN that dark time of cruel wrong, when on our country's
　　breast,
A dreary load, a ruthless code, with wasting terrors
　　press'd—
Our gentry stripp'd of land and clan, sent exiles o'er
　　the main,
To turn the scales on foreign fields for foreign
　　monarch's gain ;
Our people trod like vermin down, all fenceless flung
　　to sate
Extortion, lust, and brutal whim, and rancorous bigot
　　hate—

Our priesthood tracked from cave to hut, like felons
chased and lashed,
And from their ministering hands the lifted chalice
dashed—
In that black time of law-wrought crime, of stifling
woe and thrall,
There stood supreme one foul device, one engine
worse than all :
Him whom they wished to keep a slave, they sought
to make a brute—
They banned the light of heaven—they bade instruc-
tion's voice be mute.

God's second priest—the Teacher—sent to feed men's
mind with lore—
They marked a price upon his head, as on the priest's
before.
Well—well they knew that never, face to face beneath
the sky,
Could tyranny and knowledge meet, but one of them
must die :
That lettered slaves will link their might until their
murmurs grow
To that imperious thunder-peal which despots quail
to know ;
That men who learn will learn their strength—the
weakness of their lords—
Till all the bonds that gird them round are snapt like
Samson's cords.

This well they knew, and called the power of ignorance
  to aid :
So might, they deemed, an abject race of soulless serfs
  be made—
When Irish memories, hopes, and thoughts, were
  withered, branch and stem—
A race of abject, soulless serfs, to hew and draw for
  them.

Ah, God is good and nature strong—they let not
  thus decay
The seeds that deep in Irish breasts of Irish feeling
  lay :
Still sun and rain made emerald green the loveliest
  fields on earth,
And gave the type of deathless hope, the little shamrock, birth ;
Still faithful to their Holy Church, her direst straits
  among,
To one another faithful still, the priests and people
  clung,
And Christ was worshipped, and received with trembling haste and fear,
In field and shed, with posted scouts to warn of
  blood-hounds near ;
Still, crouching 'neath the sheltering hedge, or
  stretched on mountain fern,
The teacher and his pupils met, feloniously—to
  learn ;

Still round the peasant's heart of hearts his darling
    music twined,
A fount of Irish sobs or smiles in every note
    enshrined.
And still beside the smouldering turf were fond
    traditions told
Of heavenly saints and princely chiefs—the power
    and faith of old.

Deep lay the seeds, yet rankest weeds sprang mingled
    —could they fail?
For what were freedom's blessed worth, if slavery
    wrought not bale?
As thrall, and want and ignorance, still deep and,
    deeper grew,
What marvel weakness, gloom, and strife fell dark
    amongst us too ;
And servile thoughts, that measure not the inborn
    wealth of man—
And servile cringe, and subterfuge to 'scape our
    master's ban ;
And drunkenness—our sense of woe a little while to
    steep—
And aimless feud, and murderous plot—oh, one could
    pause and weep !
'Mid all the darkness, faith in Heaven still shone a
    saving ray,
And Heaven o'er our redemption watched, and chose
    its own good day.

Two men were sent us*—one for years, with Titan
    strength of soul,
To beard our foes, to peal our wrongs, to band us
    and control.
The other at a latter time, on gentler mission came,
To make our noblest glory spring from out our saddest
    shame!
On all our wondrous, upward course hath Heaven its
    finger set,
And we—but, oh, my countrymen, there's much before
    us yet!

How sorrowful the useless powers our glorious Island
    yields—
Our countless havens desolate, our waste of barren
    fields;
The all unused mechanic-might our rushing streams
    afford,
The buried treasures of our mines, our sea's unvalued
    hoard!
But, oh, there is one piteous waste, whence all the rest
    have grown—
One worse neglect, the mind of man left desert and
    unsown.
Send KNOWLEDGE forth to scatter wide, and deep to
    cast its seeds,
The nurse of energy and hope, of manly thoughts and
    deeds.

* It need scarcely be said that these two men were O'Connell
and Father Mathew.

Let it go forth : right soon will spring those forces in
    its train
That vanquish Nature's stubborn strength, that rifle
    earth and main—
Itself a nobler harvest far than Autumn tints with
    gold,
A. higher wealth, a surer gain than wave and mine
    enfold.
Let it go forth unstained, and purged from Pride's
    unholy leaven,
With fearless forehead raised to Man, but humbly
    bent to Heaven ;

Deep let it sink in Irish hearts the story of their
    isle,
And waken thoughts of tenderest love, and burning
    wrath the while ;
And press upon us, one by one, the fruits of English
    sway,
And blend the wrongs of bygone times with this our
    fight to-day ;
And show our Fathers' constancy by truest instinct
    led,
To loathe and battle with the power that on their
    substance fed ;
And let it place beside our own the world's vast page,
    to tell
That *never lived the nation yet could rule another
well.*

Thus, thus our cause shall gather   strength ;   no
    feeling vague and blind,
But stamped by passion on the heart, by reason on
    the mind.
Let it go forth—a mightier foe to England's power
    than all
The rifles of America—the armaments of Gaul! ·
It *shall* go forth, and woe to them that bar or thwart
    its way—
'Tis God's own light—all Heavenly bright—we care
    not who says nay.

JOHN O'HAGAN.

GIRL OF THE RED MOUTH.

GIRL of the red mouth,
    Love me ! Love me !
Girl of the red mouth,
    Love me !
'Tis by its curve, I know,
Love fashioneth his bow,
And bends it—ah, even so !
    Oh, girl of the red mouth, love me !

Girl of the blue eye,
    Love me ! Love me !
Girl of the dew eye,
    Love me !

Worlds hang for lamps on high ;
And thought's world lives in thy
Lustrous and tender eye—
    Oh, girl of the blue eye, love me !

Girl of the swan's neck,
    Love me ! Love me !
Girl of the swan's neck,
    Love me !
As a marble Greek doth grow
To his steed's back of snow,
Thy white neck sits thy shoulder so,—
    Oh, girl of the swan's neck, love me !

Girl of the low voice,
    Love me ! Love me !
Girl of the sweet voice,
    Love me !
Like the echo of a bell,—
Like the bubbling of a well—
Sweeter ! Love within doth dwell,
    Oh, girl of the low voice, love me !

MARTIN MacDermott.

MY OWEN.

PROUD of you, fond of you, clinging so near to you,
Light is my heart now I know I am dear to you;
Glad is my voice now I know it may sing for you
All the wild love that is burning within for you!
Tell me once more—tell it over and over—
The tale of that eve which first saw you my lover;
        Now I need never blush
        At my heart's hottest gush—
The wife of my Owen her heart may discover!

Proud of you, fond of you, having all right in you,
Quitting all else through my love and delight in you,
Glad is my heart since 'tis beating so nigh to you,
Light is my step for it always may fly to you!
Clasped in your arms, where no sorrow can reach to me,
Reading your eyes, till new love they shall teach to me;
        Though wild and weak till now,
        By that blest marriage vow,
More than the wisest know, your heart shall preach to me.

ELLEN MARY DOWNING

THE VOICE OF NATURE.

THE winds they sang in the boughs above,
　The waves they sang in the stream below;
They sang to my soul; and Peace and Love
　　　In their cadence fell,
　As cooling winds from the waters blow.

And I said "the light so strange and fair
　That banished the gloom in my life's dark sky,
Oh, 'twas not a rocket to burst in glare,
　　　But an arctic star—
　A light that shall never fade or die."　·

"Sweet Sybil," I said, "the summer beam
　Is type of your spirit so fresh and warm;
If fondly in peace it sparkle and gleam,　　　·
　　　Like that light of Heaven
　'Twill burn as bright through the passing storm.

" For I look in her face like nature's own,"
　(I said) "my love is so young and fair,
Till the clouds of fear, like the night have flown,
　　　And my breast is lit
　With the morning hope that is beaming there.

" And gather ye stormful clouds," I said,
　" And waken ye howling winds and roar;
I watch where that light of my life is shed
　　　For the sign that saith
　My love will love me for evermore!"

For the winds they sang in the boughs above
And the waves they sang in the stream below
And my heart so ripe for peace and love,
Into blossom burst
As roses bud in the summer glow !

CHARLES GAVAN DUFFY.

THE MOUNTAIN FERN.

[The author of this poem, who has bequeathed to us many striking and vigorous ballads, was never more happily inspired than here, except perhaps in his quaint and picturesque introduction to "The Monks of Kilcrea," first published in Petrie's *Irish Penny Journal*. Geoghegan belonged in a double sense to the confraternity of Robert Burns ; but happier in one respect than his illustrious confrere, he had risen to a high position before, at an advanced age, he retired from the service. It is pleasant to be able to add that he retained undiminished to his dying hour, in the innermost core of his heart, his love for liberty and Ireland.]

OH, the Fern ! the Fern !—the Irish hill Fern !—
That girds our blue lakes from Lough Ine* to Lough
      Erne,
That waves on our crags, like the plume of a king
And bends, like a nun, over clear well and spring !

* Lough Ine, a singularly romantic lake in the western mountains of Cork ; of Lough Erne, I hope, to Irishmen it is unneces-
sary to speak.

The fairy's tall palm tree ! the heath-bird's fresh nest,
And the couch the red deer deems the sweetest and
    best,
With the free winds to fan it, and dew-drops to gem,—
Oh, what can ye match with its beautiful stem?
From the shrine of St. Finbar, by lone Avonbuie,
To the halls of Dunluce, with its towers by the sea,
From the hill of Knockthu to the rath of Moyvore,
Like a chaplet it circles our green island o'er,—
In the bawn of the chief, by the anchorite's cell,
On the hill-top, or greenwood, by streamlet or well,
With a spell on each leaf, which no mortal can learn,*—
Oh, there never was plant like the Irish hill Fern !

Oh, the Fern ! the Fern !—the Irish hill Fern !
That shelters the weary, or wild roe, or kern,
Thro' the glens of Kilcoe rose a shout on the gale,
As the Saxons rushed forth, in their wrath, from the
    Pale,
With bandog and blood-hound, all savage to see,
To hunt thro' Clunealla the wild Rapparee !
Hark ! a cry from yon dell on the startled ear rings,
And forth from the wood the young fugitive springs,
Thro' the copse, o'er the bog, and, oh, saints be his
    guide !
His fleet step now falters—there's blood on his side !

* The fortunate discoverer of the fern seed is supposed to obtain
the power of rendering himself invisible at pleasure.

Yet onward he strains, climbs the cliff, fords the stream,
And sinks on the hill-top, mid bracken leaves green,
And thick o'er his brow are their fresh clusters piled,
And they cover his form, as a mother her child;
And the Saxon is baffled!—they never discern
Where it shelters and saves him—the Irish hill Fern!

Oh, the Fern! the Fern!—the Irish hill Fern!—
That pours a wild.keen o'er the hero's grey cairn;
Go, hear it at midnight, when stars are all out,
And the wind o'er the hillside is moaning about,
With a rustle and stir, and a low wailing tone
That thrills through the heart with its whispering lone;
And ponder its meaning, when haply you stray
Where the halls of the chieftain in ruin decay.
With night owls for warders, the goshawk for guest,
And their daïs of honour by cattle-hoofs prest—
With its fosse choked with rushes, and spider-webs
    flung,
Over walls where the marchmen their red weapons
    hung,
With a curse on their name, and a sigh for the hour
That tarries so long—look! what waves on the tower?
With an omen and sign, and an augury stern,
'Tis the *Green Flag* of Time!—'tis the Irish hill Fern!

ARTHUR G. GEOGHEGAN.

THE EXILE'S DEVOTION.

If I forswear the art divine
    That glorifies the dead—
What comfort then can I call mine,
    What solace seek instead?
For, from my birth, our country's fame
    Was life to me and love;
And for each loyal Irish name
    Some garland still I wove.

I'd rather be the bird that sings
    Above the martyr's grave,
Than fold in fortune's cage my wings
    And feel my soul a slave;
I'd rather turn one simple verse
    True to the Gaelic ear
Than sapphic odes I might rehearse
    With senates listening near.

Oh, native land! dost ever mark
    When the world's din is drown'd
Betwixt the day-light and the dark,
    A wandering solemn sound
That on the western wind is borne
    Across thy dewy breast?
It is the Voice of those who mourn
    For thee, far in the West!

For them and theirs I oft essay
  Your ancient art of Song,
And often sadly turn away,
  Deeming my rashness wrong;
For well I ween, a loving will
  Is all the art I own :—
Ah me! could love suffice for skill,
  What triumphs I had known!

My native land! my native land!
  Live in my memory still!—
Break on my brain, ye surges grand!
  Stand up, mist-cover'd hill!
Still on the mirror of the mind
  The scenes I love, I see:
Would I could fly on the western wind,
  My native land, to thee!

THOMAS D'ARCY McGEE.

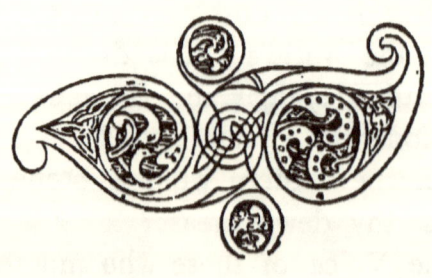

THE OLD STORY.

"Old as the universe, yet not outworn."—The Island.

He came across the meadow-pass,
   That summer-eve of eves,
The sunlight streamed along the grass,
   And glanced amid the leaves;
And from the shrubbery below,
   And from the garden trees,
He heard the thrushes' music flow,
   And humming of the bees;
The garden-gate was swung apart—
   The space was brief between;
But there, for throbbing of his heart,
   He paused perforce to lean.

He leaned upon the garden-gate;
   He looked, and scarce he breathed;
Within the little porch she sate,
   With woodbine overwreathed;
Her eyes upon her work was bent
   Unconscious who was nigh;
But oft the needle slowly went,
   And oft did idle lie;
And ever to her lips arose
   Sweet fragments faintly sung,
But ever, ere the notes could close,
   She hushed them on her tongue.

Her fancies as they come and go
　　Her pure face speaks the while,
For now it is a flitting glow,
　　And now a breaking smile;
And now it is a graver shade
　　When holier thoughts are there—
An angel's pinion might be stayed
　　To see a sight so fair;
But still they hid her looks of light,
　　Those downcast eyelids pale—
Two lovely clouds so silken white,
　　Two lovelier stars that veil.

The sun at length his burning edge
　　Had rested on the hill,
And save one thrush from out the hedge
　　Both bower and grove were still.
The sun had almost bade farewell;
　　But one reluctant ray
Still loved within that porch to dwell
　　As charmèd there to stay—
It stole aslant the pear-tree bough,
　　And through the woodbine fringe,
And kissed the maiden's neck and brow,
　　And bathed her in its tinge.

Oh! beauty of my heart, he said,
　　Oh! darling, darling mine,
Was ever light of evening shed
　　On loveliness like thine?

Why should I ever leave this spot,
    But gaze until I die ?
A moment from that bursting thought
    She felt his footstep nigh.
One sudden lifted glance—but one,
    A tremor and a start,
So gently was their greeting done
    That who would guess their heart ?

Long, long the sun had sunken down,
    And all his golden trail
Had died away to lines of brown,
    In duskier hues that fail.
The grasshopper was chirping shrill—
    No other living sound
Accompanied the tiny rill
    That gurgled under ground—
No other living sound, unless
    Some spirit bent to hear
Low words of human tenderness,
    And mingling whispers near.

The stars, like pallid gems at first,
    Deep in the liquid sky,
Now forth upon the darkness burst,
    Sole kings and lights on high
In splendour, myriad-fold, supreme—
    No rival moonlight strove,
Nor lovelier e'er was Hesper's beam,
    Nor more majestic Jove.

But what if hearts there beat that night
  That recked not of the skies,
Or only felt their imaged light
  In one another's eyes?

And if two worlds of hidden thought
  And fostered passion met,
Which, passing human language, sought
  And found an utterance yet;
And if they trembled like to flowers
  That droop across a stream,
The while the silent starry hours
  Glide o'er them like a dream;
And if, when came the parting time,
  They faltered still and clung;
What is it all?—an ancient rhyme
  Ten thousand times besung—
That part of Paradise which man
  Without the portal knows—
Which hath been since the world began,
  And shall be till its close.

JOHN O'HAGAN.

BLESS THE DEAR OLD VERDANT LAND!

BLESS the dear old verdant land!
  Brother, wert thou born of it?
As thy shadow life doth stand
Twining round its rosy band,
Did an Irish mother's hand
  Guide thee in the morn of it?
Did a father's first command
  Teach thee love or scorn of it?

Thou who treadst its fertile breast
  Dost thou feel a glow for it?
Thou of all its charms possest,
Living on its first and best,
Art thou but a thankless guest,
  Or a traitor foe for it?
If thou lovest, where's the test?
  Wilt thou strike a blow for it?

Has the past no goading sting
  That can make thee rouse for it
Does thy land's reviving spring,
Full of buds and blossoming,
Fail to make thy cold heart cling—
  Breathing lover's vows for it?
With the circling ocean's ring
  Thou wert made a spouse for

Hast thou kept as thou shouldst keep
  Thy affections warm for it—
Letting no cold feeling creep
Like an ice-breath o'er the deep
Freezing to a stony sleep.
  Hopes the heart would form for it—
Glories that like rainbows peep
  Thro' the darkening storm for it!

Son of this down-trodden land,
  Aid us in the fight for it.
We seek to make it great and grand,
Its shipless bays—its naked strand—
By canvas-swelling breezes fanned:
  Oh what a glorious sight for it!
The past expiring like a brand
  In morning's rosy light for it!

Think, this dear old land is thine—
  And thou a traitor slave of it—
Think how the Switzer leads his kine,
When pale the evening star doth shine;
His song has home in every line—
  Freedom in every stave of it!
Think how the German loves his Rhine,
  And worships every wave of it!

Our own dear land is bright as theirs;
  But oh! our hearts are cold for it;
Awake! we are not slaves but heirs.
Our fatherland requires our cares—

Our speech with men, with God our prayers ;
Spurn blood-stained Judas gold for it—
Let us do all that honour dares—
Be earnest, faithful, bold for it!

DENIS FLORENCE MACCARTHY.

THE DEATH OF O'CAROLAN.

[Thorlogh O'Carolan, born at Nobber, A.D. 1670, became
blind at the age of manhood, and then the harp which had been
his amusement became his profession. The lady of The
Macdermott, of Aldersford in Roscommon, equipped him with
horse, harp, and *gossoon*. At every house he was a welcome
guest, and for half a century he wandered from mansion to
mansion improvising words and airs. Roscommon, the native
county of Goldsmith, was his favourite district, where he died in
1731, at the house of his first patroness. One of Goldsmith's
most touching essays is on "Carolan the Blind," concerning
whom, no doubt, many a tale was current on the country-side in
Goldsmith's young days; and his musical influence can certainly
be traced not only in Goldsmith's Poems, but also in Sheridan,
Moore and Gerald Griffin.—Author's Note.]

THERE is an empty seat by many a board,
A guest is miss'd in hostelry and hall—
There is a harp hung up in Alderford
That was, in Ireland, sweetest harp of all.
The hand that made it speak, woe's me ! is cold,
The darken'd eye-balls roll inspired no more ;
The lips— the potent lips—gape like a mould
Where late the golden torrent floated o'er.

In vain the watchman looks from Mayo's towers
  For him whose presence filled all hearts with mirth ;
In vain the gather'd guests outsit the hours—
  The honour'd chair is vacant by the hearth.
From Castle Archdall, Moneyglass and Trim,
  The courteous messages go forth in vain ;
Kind words no longer have a joy for him
  Whose final lodge is in Death's dark demesne !

Kilronan Abbey is his castle now,
  And there, till Doomsday, peacefully he'll stay.
In vain they weave new garlands for his brow,
  In vain they go to meet him by the way ;
In kindred company, he does not tire—
  The native dead and noble lie around ;
His life-long song has ceased, his wood and wire
  Rest, a sweet harp unstrung, in holy ground.

Last of our ancient minstrels ! thou, who lent
  A buoyant motive to a foundering race—
Whose saving song, into their being blent,
  Sustained them by its passion and its grace :
God rest you ! may your judgment dues be light,
  Dear Thorlogh ! and the purgatorial days
Be few and short, till clothed in holy white,
  Your soul may come before the throne of rays.

THOMAS D'ARCY McGEE.

OLD LOVE AND NEW.

My old love! his hazel eyes
  Were very dark and fine,
And very conscious did they look
  A-bending down to mine:
My new love—my new love—
  It is not shape or hue,
But your eyes have that would lure my heart
  The world to wander through!

My old love was smooth of tongue,
  And soft he spoke and well;
I asked my heart what more it sought?
  It sighed and could not tell.
My new love—my new love—
  What magic could it be,
That made me, in your first few words,
  Such difference to see?

The while I loved my old love
  I walk'd amid my flowers,
And fed my thoughts with passion's lays—
  Such love, said I, is ours:
My new love—my new love—
  Was never verse or tale—
Could e'er interpret what I feel,
  Or solace what I ail.

My old love—my fancy dwelt
  Upon him when away ;
But, with him, still I felt a void
  And why, I could not say.
My new love ! my new love !
  Beside you, when I rest,
My cheek is like the western heaven,
  And heaven itself my breast.

Farewell, farewell, my old love—
  Your heart will never break,
Though sore your pride be mortified
  And I the blame must take.
But if I broke a thousand hearts—
  If all the world cried shame—
My new love ! my true love !
  I'd love you all the same.

JOHN O'HAGAN

THE COOLUN.

THE scene is beside where the Avon-mor flows —
'Tis the spring of the year, and the day's near its
 close ;
And an old woman sits with a boy on her knee—
She smiles like the evening, and *he*, like the lea !
Her hair is as white as the flax ere it's spun,
His, brown as yon beech that is· hiding the sun.
    Beside the bright river,
    The calm, glassy river,
   That's sliding, and gliding all peacefully on.

"Come, granny," the boy says, "you'll sing me, I
 know,
The beautiful *Coolun*, so sweet and so low ;
For I love its soft tones more than blackbird or thrush,
Though often the tears in a shower will gush
From my eyes, when I hear it. Dear granny, say why,
When my heart's full of gladness, I sob and I cry
    To hear the sweet Coolun,
    The beautiful Coolun—
   An angel first sang it above in the sky !"

And *she* sings, and *he* listens ; but many years pass,
And the old woman sleeps 'neath the chapel-yard grass ;
And a couple are seated upon the same stone
Where the boy sat and listened so oft to the crone :—

'Tis the boy—'tis the man ! and he says while he sighs
To the girl by his side with the love-streaming eyes :—
"Oh sing me, sweet Oona,
My beautiful Oona,
Oh, sing me the Coolun," he says and he sighs.

"That air, mo stor, brings back the days of my youth,
That flowed like the river there, sunny and smooth ;
And it brings back the old woman, kindly and dear—
If her spirit, dear Oona, is hovering near,
'Twill glad her to hear the old melody rise
Warm, warm, on the wings of our love and our sighs—
Oh, sing me the Coolun,
The beautiful Coolun,"—
Is't the dew, or a tear-drop, is moist'ing his eyes ?

There's a change on the scene,—far more grand but
    less fair,
By the broad-rolling Hudson are seated the pair;
And the gray hemlock-fir waves its branches above,
As they sigh for their land, as they murmur their love ;
Hush ! the heart hath been touched, and its musical
    strings
Vibrate into song ! 'tis the Coolun she sings—
The home-sighing Coolun,
The love-breathing Coolun,
A well for all memory's deep flowing springs.

They think of the bright stream they sat down beside,
When he was a bridegroom, and she was his bride;

The pulses of youth seem to throb in the strain,—
Old faces, long vanished, look kindly again,—
Kind voices float round them, and grand hills are near,
Their feet have not touched, ah, this many a year!
And as ceases the Coolun,
The home-breathing Coolun,
Not the air, but their native land, faints on the ear.

Long in silence they weep, with hand claspèd in hand,
Then to God send up pray'rs for the far-off old land;
And while grateful to Him for the blessings He's sent,
They know 'tis His hand that withholdeth content :—
For the Exile and Christian must evermore sigh
For the home upon earth, and the home in the sky—
So they sing the sweet Coolun,
The sorrowful Coolun,
That murmurs of both homes,—they sing and they sigh.

A BENEDICTION.

Heaven bless thee, old Bard, in whose bosom were
nursed
Emotions that into each melody burst!
Be thy grave ever green! may the softest of showers
And brightest of beams nurse its grass and its flowers.
Oft, oft, be it moist with the tear-drop of love—
And may angels watch round thee for ever above,
Old bard of the Coolun!
The beautiful Coolun,
That sobs, like dear Eirè, with Sorrow and Love.

MARTIN MACDERMOTT.

O'DONOVAN'S DAUGHTER.

[The three following songs were evidently written in praise
of the same young beauty. The first sings the joy of the
meeting ; the second and third, alas, are devoted to the regrets
of the parting of the lovers.]

AIR—"*Juice of the Barley.*"

ONE midsummer's eve, when the Bel-fires were lighted,
And the bag-piper's tune called the maidens delighted,
I joined a gay group by the Araglyn's[1] water,
And danced till the dawn with O'Donovan's daughter.

Have you seen the ripe monadan[2] glisten in Kerry ?
Have you marked on the Galtees the black whortle-
      berry ?
Or ceanabhan[3] wave by the walls of Blackwater ?
They're the cheek, eye, and neck of O'Donovan's
      daughter ?

Have you watched a wild kidling[4] on Claragh's round
      mountain ?
The swan's arching glory on Sheeling's blue fountain ?
Heard a weird woman chant what the fairy choir
      taught her ?
They've the step, grace and love of O'Donovan's
      daughter.

(1) A stream in the western part of the barony of Duhallow,
Co. Cork.

(2) The cranberry, met with only on the wildest mountains.

(3) Ceanabhan, pron. : canavan, the beautiful pendulus cotton-
plant of the bogs.

(4) Claragh, a romantic hill.   Co. Cork.

Have you marked in its flight the black wing of the
    raven?
The rose-buds that breathe in the summer-breeze
    waven?
The pearls that lie hid under Lene's[5] magic water?
They're the teeth, lips and hair of O'Donovan's
    daughter.

Ere the Bel-fire was dimm'd, or the dancers departed,
I taught her a song of some maid broken-hearted;
And that group, and that dance, and that love-song
    I taught her
Haunt my slumber at night with O'Donovan's daughter.

God grant 'tis no fay from Cnoc-Firinn[6] that woos me!
God grant 'tis not Cliodhna[7] the queen that pursues me!
That my soul lost and lone has no witchery wrought me,
While I dream of dark groves with O'Donovan's
    daughter!

If spell-bound I pine with an airy disorder,
Saint Gobnate has sway over Musgry's[8] white border,
She'll scare from my couch, when with prayer I've
    besought her,
That bright airy sprite like O'Donovan's daughter!

EDWARD WALSH.

[5] Lake of Killarney.

[6] A celebrated fairy-hill in the Co. Limerick, the residence
of Doun, king of the fairies of West Munster.

[7] Cliodhna, or Cleena, the fairy queen of South Munster,
much given to the abduction of young men.

[8] A territory extending from Dripsey to Ballyvoorney, Co.
Cork.

THERE'S A GLEN OF GREEN BEAUTY.

THERE'S a glen of green beauty, where echoes have
 spoken,
 And waters of brightness o'er rude rocks are flung.
In the glen blooms a bower, but haply 'tis broken
 Where Mary the strains of her poet oft sung.
Till memory dies in the breast of the weeper,
 Those moments of rapture he'll never forget;
Tho' vanish'd for aye, like the dream of the sleeper,—
 I wonder does Mary remember them yet?

Oh, ne'er shall the bard in that green blooming bower
 Hear Mary's voice warble his wild song again—
For young hearts that trembled to passion's soft power
 Misfortune for ever hath sundered in twain!
As bright eyes may light him o'er life's troubled ocean
 As kind may caress him—but can he forget
The raptures that hallow the heart's first devotion—
 I wonder does Mary remember them yet?

Restore him the bloom of a hope early blighted!
 Efface from his heart the deep trace of despair!
Recall that wild vow which to heaven he once
 plighted!
 Bid his soul be as pure as when first love was
 there!

Oh, never shall peace to his dark soul be spoken,
  Or his couch be unstained with the tears of regret,
For pleasures long vanished and tender ties broken—
  I wonder does Mary remember them yet?

EDWARD WALSH.

A BIRD IN THE DEEP VALLEY SINGING.

THERE'S a bird in the deep valley singing,
  That charms with his soft vesper song;
And a flow'ret, thrice beautiful, springing
  The fairest the valleys among.
But the primrose might flourish forsaken,
  The thrush vainly sing from his tree,
If Mary were there to awaken
  Her wild note of sweetness for me.

O'er the rocks is the bright water sweeping;
  Below, waves the green alder grove;
Yon cliff holds the wild echoes sleeping,
  That oft woke to songs that I love.
The moonlight of magical power
  Still streams through the old trysting tree;
But Mary, fair star of that bower,
  Hath fled from the valley and me.

We met—and have parted for ever;
We loved,—but howe'er be *her* heart,
From mine shall the memory never
Of beautiful Mary depart.
Nor canst thou, O'Donovan's daughter !
Permit from remembrance to flee
The twilight—the rush of wild water—
The bright star—the bower—and me.

EDWARD WALSH.

THOMAS DAVIS'S UNPUBLISHED VERSES

[In Sir Charles Gavan Duffy's "Memoir of Thomas Davis" some unpublished poems of his are given which ought to find a place here. Although probably these verses did not receive his final corrections, they are precious as being the last written by Ireland's most cherished poet. The following all refer to the person and the scenes—both the very dearest to his heart—which inspired the lyrics given earlier in the present volume.]

I. LOVE.

REFRESHENED and uncloyed, they are springing out
    again—
The passions of my boyhood, like lions from a den ;
There are crowns upon the bramble, and angels
    among men,
And triumph in each ramble, and fairies in each glen.

I rush across the mountain, twice wilder than the
    wind ;
I squander, without counting, the money of my
    mind ;
All hands have pleasant pressure, all voices sing a
    song—
The world was made for pleasure, and it cannot
    last too long.

And what has changed my being, and what baptized
    my heart
That, mid old sorrows fleeing, my lightning spirits
    dart ?
And why this cherub chorus ?—and why this hovering
    dove—
Peace round, within and o'er us?—Sweet sweetheart
    it is love.

2. THE CHANGE.

I USED to sing of war and peace,
    Of heroes dead and buried ;
Of Ireland's wrongs forbid to cease
    Until her sons were serried ;
But now I've not a fiery thought,
    Nor rhymes, who had so many.
My soul is soft ; my heart is caught ;
    I only sing of Annie.

Now, if I read of ancient days,
  Or search through storied regions
'Tis but to swell romantic lays,
  Or mould beguiling legends.
Nay, if I sit and hear the wind
  Pour through a castle's cranny,
I only seek sweet sounds to find
And weave in songs for Annie.

And yet, *machree*, were we not fond
  Of freedom and Old Eirinn ;
Were we not fretted by each bond
  Our countrymen are wearing ;
Were we not full of hope to see
  Our country great as any,
Methinks the power would pass from me
  To sing for even Annie !

3. ANNIE IN THE SOUTH.

WOULD I were now thy guide,
          Annie dear,
Where across Munster wide,
          Annie dear,
Cliff-guarded rivers glide,
Lakes in the mountain hide,
'Towers topple o'er the tide,
          Annie dear.

To glance down the silver Nore,
     Annie dear,
Whisper till day was o'er,
     Annie dear,
Tenderly lead thee through
Soft winding Avondhu—
Softer 'twould seem for you
     Annie dear.

Fairest! I'd show you there,
     Annie dear,
Brave men and maidens fair,
     Annie dear;
Never a nobler racc!
Sweet tongue and gentle grace—
Often how sad the face,
     Annie dear.

Then would you list me tell,
     Annie dear,
How their sad fate befell,
     Annie dear,
Faith to a foreign king—
Feuds thick as leaves in spring,
Oh, 'twould your bosom wring,
     Annie dear!

Then, we would haste away,
          Annie dear,
Off to lone Ceim-an-Eich,
          Annie dear,
Wander in Finbar's isle,—
Was it a maiden's wile
Drove him to that defile,
          Annie dear?

Lone, in some gliding boat,
          Annie dear,
Off from Glengariff float,
          Annie dear;
List to the ocean's sighs,
Look on the purple skies,—
Look in each other's eyes,
          Annie dear!

Holding your bridle rein,
          Annie dear,
Arran's steep ridge we'd gain,
          Annie dear;
Never was view so fair,
Island, lake, hill and air,—
Dream a long day-dream there,
          Annie dear.

Long silent echoes wake,
                Annie dear,
Circling Killarney's lake,
                Annie dear;
Mingling wild minstrelsy,
Legend and history,
Pondering love's mystery,
                Annie dear.

Oh, that it ne'er would end,
                Annie dear;
Sweet 'twere such life to spend,
                Annie dear;
Then like an angel dance,
Ending in holy trance,—
Ah! 'tis a wild romance!
                Annie dear.

4. ANNIE AWAY.

HER hair it is the trees at night;
  Her forehead is the moon;
Her eyes they are a nameless light;
  Her heart a tender tune.
We told each other to forget,
  As if we thought we should;
'Twas said we might not wed, and yet
  We kissed as if we could.

They said 'twas good for us to part,
  Nor, maybe, meet again;
Or if we met, her callow heart
  Might well be changed, ere then.
They knew not Annie as I knew,
  For all their kindly fear;
For all our sad and strange adieu,
  You'll wed me, Annie dear.

5. MY ANNIE.

So gentle and joyous, the cloud floating by
Doesn't sail half so gracefully over the sky;
And the sun in the flower-bedded dewdrop that lies
Is common and cold to the love in her eyes.

Oh, heaven, such a heart! and to think that it's mine
To think, when I'm absent, that sweet heart will pine!
To think that she pants when my footstep is near!
And dreams of my breast as a refuge from fear.

My God, look upon her! how good and how fair!
And charge the good angels to make her their care;
And grant that our grey hairs may mingle below
Ere our souls close together to Paradise go.

THOMAS DAVIS.

THE OLD CHURCH AT LISMORE.

[This poem, inscribed in the MS., "My Last Verses," was the last written by "Mary" before entering on her novitiate in 1849.]

OLD Church, thou still art Catholic !—e'en dream
    they as they may
That the new rites and worship have swept the
    old away ;
There is no form of beauty raised by nature, or by art,
That preaches not God's saving truths to man's
    adoring heart !

In vain they tore the altar down ; in vain they
    flung aside
The mournful emblem of the death which our sweet
    Saviour died ;
In vain they left no single trace of saint or angel here—
Still angel-spirits haunt the ground, and to the soul
    appear.

I marvel how, in scenes like these, so coldly they can
    pray,
Nor hold sweet commune with the dead who once
    knelt down as they ;
Yet not as they, in sad mistrust or sceptic doubt
    —for, oh,
They looked in hope to the blessèd saints, these
    dead of long ago.

And, then, the churchyard, soft and calm, spread
    out beyond the scene,
With sunshine warm and soothing shade and trees
    upon its green ;
Ah ! though their cruel Church forbid, are there
    no hearts will pray
For the poor souls that trembling left that cold
    and speechless clay ?

My God ! I am a Catholic ! I grew into the ways
Of my dear Church since first my voice could lisp
    a word of praise ;
But oft I think, though my first youth were taught
    and trained awrong,
I still had learnt the one true faith from nature and
    from song !

For still, whenever dear friends die, it is such joy
    to know
They are not all beyond the care that healed their
    wounds below ;
That we can pray them into peace, and speed
    them to the shore
Where clouds and cares and thorny griefs shall
    vex their hearts no more.

And the sweet saints, so meek below, so merciful
    above ;
And the pure angels, watching still with such un-
    tiring love ;

And the kind Virgin, Queen of Heaven, with all
　　her mother's care,
Who prays for earth, because she knows what
　　breaking hearts are there !

Oh, let us lose no single link that our dear Church
　　has bound,
To keep our hearts more close to Heaven, on earth's
　　ungenial ground ;
But trust in saint and martyr yet, and o'er their
　　hallowed clay,
Long after we have ceased to weep, kneel faithful
　　down to pray.

So shall the land for us be still the Sainted Isle of
　　old,
Where hymn and incense rise to Heaven, and holy
　　beads are told ;
And even the ground they tore from God, in years
　　of crime and woe,
Instinctive with His truth and love, shall breathe
　　of long ago !

ELLEN MARY DOWNING.

PROTESTANT ASCENDANCY.

[" A Protestant King, a Protestant House of Lords and Commons, a Protestant Hierarchy ; the courts of justice, the army, the navy, and the revenue, in all their branches and details, Protestant—and this system fortified and maintained by a connexion with the Protestant State of Great Britain :—

" The Protestants of Ireland will never relinquish their political position, which their fathers won with their swords, and which they, therefore, regard as their birthright."—*Letter of the Dublin Corporation*, 1793.]

GREAT fabric of oppression
  By tyrant plunderers planned,
So giant-vast, so iron-fast,
That were not God's great fiat pass'd,
That man's injustice shall not last
  Thou might'st eternal stand ;
Black fortress of ascendancy,
  Beneath whose wasting sway
Sprang crime and strife, so deadly rife—
  What rests of thee to-day?

A few unsightly fragments,
  The scoff and scorn of all,
Long pierc'd and rent by Freedom's power
They rot and crumble hour by hour,
And wait the lightest storm to lour,
  In hapless wreck to fall.

What show of faded banners,
　　What shouts of angry men,
Or doughty threat, or sullen fret,
　　Will raise that pile again ?

Vain ! vain ! go seek the charnel
　　Where haughty Clare lies low ;
Tell him how ruin darkens o'er
The cause he sav'd in flames and gore,
How his strong will is needed sore
　　In· this your day of woe—
Rouse bloody Toler, summon all
　　Clan Beresford to gorge and prey,
And acrid Saurin's heart of gall
　　And serpent Castlereagh.
And those dry bones shall hearken
　　And smite with ghastly fear
This isle once more, ere ye restore
　　Their dead dominion here.

Vain ! vain ! can ye roll backward
　　The world for fifty years ?
From thrice three glowing millions drain
Their strength and substance, heart and brain ;
Where thought and daring impulse reign,
　　Plant old derided fears ?
Get their strong limbs your yoke to bear
　　Your grasp upon their purse ?

Your maddest madman would not dare
    So wild a dream to nurse—
Awake! awake! your paths to take
    For better or for worse.

The better lies before you,
    The noblest ever trod ;
To meet your brothers face to face,
Quell idle feuds of creed or race,
And take your gallant grandsires' place
    To free your native sod.
Make recreant statesmen tremble
    And ingrate England quail,
And win and wear the proudest share
    In Ireland's proudest tale.

The worse—'tis yours to choose it—
    In helpless rage to stand :
To see the gulf and trembling wait—
To writhe beneath o'ermastering fate,
Repelling with a scowl of hate
    Your brother's outstretched hand.
In history known as tigers
    Whose teeth and fangs were drawn,
Whose heart and will were murderous still
    When means and strength were gone.

Know, Protestants of Ireland,
　　That, doomed among mankind—
Marked with the fatal mark, are they
Who will not know their place or day,
But cling to phantoms pass'd away,
　　And sow the barren wind.
Life's ever-shifting currents
　　Brave men put forth to try,
They wait beside the ebbing tide
　　Till darkness finds them dry.

JOHN O'HAGAN.

TIPPERARY.

WERE you ever in sweet Tipperary, where the fields
　　are so sunny and green,
And the heath-brown Slieve-bloom and the Galtees
　　look down with so proud a mien?
'Tis there you would see more beauty than is on all
　　Irish ground—
God bless you, my sweet Tipperary, for where could
　　your match be found?

They say that your hand is fearful, that darkness is
　　in your eye:
But I'll not let them dare to talk so black and
　　bitter a lie.

Oh! no, *macushla storin!* bright, bright, and warm
    are you,
With hearts as bold as the men of old, to yourselves
    and your country true.

Oh! come for a while among us, and give us
    the friendly hand,
And you'll see that old Tipperary is a loving and
    gladsome land;
From Upper to Lower Ormond, bright welcomes
    and smiles will spring—
On the plains of Tipperary the stranger is like a king!

MRS. VARIAN.

EXILES FAR AWAY.

WHEN round the festive Christmas board, or by
the Christmas hearth,
That glorious mingled draught is pour'd—wine,
melody, and mirth !
When friends long absent tell, low-toned, their joys
and sorrows o'er,
And hand grasps hand, and eyelids fill, and lips
meet lips once more—
Oh ! in that hour 'twere kindly done, some
woman's voice would say—
" Forget not those who're sad to-night—poor exiles
far away ! "

Alas, for them ! this morning's sun saw many a
moist eye pour
Its gushing love, with longings vain, the waste
Atlantic o'er ;
And when he turned his lion-eye this ev'ning from
the West,
The Indian shores were lined with those who
watched his couchèd crest ;
But not to share his glory then, or gladden in his ray,
They bent their gaze upon his path—those exiles far
away.

It was—oh! how the heart will cheat! because
    they thought, beyond
His glowing couch lay that Green Isle of which
    their hearts were fond;
And fancy brought old scenes of home back to
    each welling eye,
And through each breast pour'd many a thought
    that filled it, like a sigh!
'Twas then—'twas then, all warm with love, they
    knelt them down to pray
For Irish homes, and kith, and kin—poor exiles far
    away!

And then the mother bless'd her son, the lover
    bless'd the maid,
And then the soldier was a child, and wept the
    whilst he prayed,
And then the student's pallid cheek flushed red
    as summer rose,
And patriot souls forget their grief to weep for Erin's
    woes;
And, oh! but then warm vows were breathed, that
    come what might or may,
They'd right the suffering isle they loved—those
    exiles far away!

And some there were, around the board like loving
    brothers met,
The few fond faithful joyous hearts, that never can
    forget;

They pledged—"The girls we left at home, God
    bless them!" and they gave
"The memory of our absent friends, the tender and
    the brave!"
Then up, erect, with nine times nine, and hip, hip,
    hip hurrah!
Drank, "*Eirè do slainthe geal go brah !*—those exiles
    far away!

And, oh! to hear the sweet old strains of Irish music
    rise,
Like gushing memories of home, beneath far foreign
    skies,
Beneath the spreading calabash, beneath the trellised
    vine,
The bright Italian myrtle bower, or dark Canadian
    pine—
Oh, don't those old familiar strains—so sad now—
    now so gay—
Speak out your very, very hearts—poor exiles far
    away!

But heavens! how many sleep afar, all heedless of
    these strains—
Tired wanderers! who sought repose through
    Europe's battle-plains;
In strong, fierce, headlong fight they fell—as ships
    . go down in storms—
They fell, and *human* whirlwinds swept across their
    shattered forms!

No shroud, but glory, wrapped them round; nor
 prayer, nor tear, had they,
Save the wandering winds and the heavy clouds
 —poor exiles ·far away!

And might the singer claim a sigh, he too could
 tell how, tost
Upon the stranger's dreary shore, his heart's best
 hopes were lost—
How he, too, pined to hear the tones of friendship
 greet his ear,
And pined, to walk the river side, to youthful
 musing dear,
And pined, with yearning, silent love, amongst *his
 own* to stay—
Alas! it is so sad to be an exile far away!

Then, when round the Christmas board, or by the
 Christmas hearth,
That glorious mingled draught is poured—wine,
 melody, and mirth!
When friends long absent tell, low-toned, their joys
 and sorrows o'er,
And hand grasps hand, and eyelids fill, and lips
 press lips once more—
In that bright hour, perhaps — perhaps — some
 woman's voice would say—
"Think—think on those who weep to-night—poor
 exiles far away!"

MARTIN MacDermott.

TO A FRIEND GOING TO EUROPE.

OH, Pilgrim, if you bring me from the far off lands
 a sign,
Let it be some token telling of the green old land,
 once mine ;
A shell from the shores of Ireland would be dearer
 far to me
Than all the wines of the Rhine-land, or the arts of
 Italy.

For I was born in Ireland—I glory in the name—
I weep for all her woes, I remember all her fame ;
And still my heart must hope I may yet repose
 at rest
On the holy Zion of my youth, in the Israel of
 the west.

Her beauteous face is furrowed with sorrow's streamy
 rains,
Her lovely limbs are manacled with slavery's ancient
 chains ;
Yet, Pilgrim, pass not over with heedless heart or eye
The island of the gifted, of men who knew how to die.

Like the crater of a fire-mount, all without is bleak
 and bare,
But the muttering of its lips show what fire and
 force are there ;

Even now in the heaving crater, far from the gazer's
    ken,
The fiery hail is forging that will crush her foes again.

Then, Pilgrim, if you bring me from the far-off lands
    a sign,
Let it be some token telling of the green old land
    once mine ;
A shell from the shores of Ireland would be dearer
    far to me
Than all the wines of the Rhine-land, or the arts of
    Italy.

                THOMAS D'ARCY McGEE.

SONG OF THE IRISH MINSTREL.

I HEAR cold voices saying that she, my queen, is dead,
And these sad chords may never more their tones of
    music shed ;
That I, who wildly loved her, must weep in mute
    despair—
Ah, they know not how true love will cling, though
    blight and death be there !

Yes ! pale one, in thy sorrow—yes ! wronged one,
    in thy pain—
This heart has still a beat for thee, this trembling
    hand a strain ;

They cannot steal the golden store the past has left
    to me,
Or make me shrink, with broken faith, asthore
    machre! from thee.

Oh, hear, my darling, hear me!—'tis no cold pulse
    meets your own;
Its burning throbs would warm to life, though thou
    wert changed to stone!
I'll call the colour to thy cheek, the light into thine
    eye—
I know at least, if thou art dead, *my* love can never
    die.

'Twill make the air around thee warm with breath of
    living flame;
In life, or death, in joy or woe, 'twill cling to thee the
    same;
Oh, never in the gladdest hour, when thou wert proud
    and strong,
Was deeper worship poured than now, in this low
    mourning song.

               MRS. KEVIN O'DOHERTY.*

        * " Eva."

TO JESSY.

[These verses, which have been somewhat abridged, are the heart-felt expression of a real and lasting passion. Long years after they were written, when the poet was hastening to an early grave on the banks of the Mississippi, the lines which follow them, entitled, "A BREEZE THROUGH THE FOREST," were composed. They prove the persistent fidelity with which Richard D'Alton Williams clung to the love, the sorrow, and the patriotism of his early years.—ED.]

DEAREST! since we parted, sighs
Amid my gayest moments rise,
And the summer in thine eyes
    Haunts me night and day, Jessy.
Still I see the tresses flow
O'er thy bosom's globes of snow.
And thy lips before me glow
    Whereso'er I stray, Jessy.

Oh, must I wear a hopeless chain,
And force my heart, with ceaseless pain,
To throb and burn and bleed in vain,
    And ne'er to think of thee, Jessy.
Alas, I feel it tenfold glow—
Its pulses' rise, its springtide flow—
It bursts away with one wild throe,
    And flies thy slave to be, Jessy.

Oh! would thine eyes speak hope to me,
Fore Heaven, I vow, on bended knee,
With faithful heart to cherish thee
    Thro' life's tempestuous blast, Jessy.
And while the waves around us roar,
Their rage shall but unite us more,
Until, on death's mysterious shore,
    We furl our sails at last, Jessy.

My harp shall gain a sweeter string,
And learn at length of love to sing;
I'll plume my spirit's folded wing,
    And fly with thee above, Jessy.
I bear no monsters on my shield,
'Tis blank, save where, on verdant field,
The harp in Irish yew concealed,
    Shows sorrow linked with song, Jessy.

But nobler far, a soul of flame,
To Heaven that soars, from Heaven that came,
A generous heart, a guiltless fame,
    To poets still belong, Jessy.
And if I am, indeed, a bard,
Immortal song, uncrown'd, unstarr'd—
Tho' pride, and gold, and rivals guard—
    Will win thee spite of fate, Jessy.

G

Yet vain e'en music to express
Love's hopes, and fears, and keen distress,
I cannot love thee more nor less—
    I cannot fight nor fly, Jessy.
May Heaven if mine thou canst not be,
From life and love the mourner free,
And grant, who may not live for thee,
    At least for thee to die, Jessy.

              RICHARD D'ALTON WILLIAMS.

A BREEZE THROUGH THE FOREST.

THE sounding forest towers
Through the tinted blossom showers—
Green heavens raining flowers,
    Like my heart in the days that are gone.

O thousand-pillared shrine
Of an Architect divine!
What chancel meet as thine
    For praise to the days that are gone?

But oh! what forest hath
Such unforgotten path
As the haunted fairy rath
    Where we met in the days that are gone?

For an Irish Venus there,
Twining shamrocks in her hair,
Smiled a glory through the air
    Pure as dawn in the days that are gone.

Oh! the soul within her eyes,
And our mingled tears and sighs—
Hush! in Irish clay she lies;
    Hang a pall o'er the days that are gone.

Now a wailing phantom there
Wrings the death-dew from her hair,
Gazing westwards in despair
    Through the mist, where the black ships have gone.

Thou shalt not long alone.
O'er our joys abandoned throne
To the midnight breezes moan
    O'er the hopes of the days that are gone.

My life is ebbing fast,
On the fiery southern blast
I spring to thee at last,
    First love of the days that are gone.

Prophetic shadows loom
O'er my spirit from the tomb—
In glory, or in gloom,
    Thou art mine, by the days that are gone

There too the white-thorn blows
O'er the mother's dust, whose woes
One heart—one only—knows ;
    Child of tears, it is well thou art gone.

As I bore thee home to die,
The lark filled all the sky ;
'Twas thine angel's call on high—
    Let us pray for the souls that are ᴇ

I miss the cloister bells
Through the ruin-hallowed dells,
The round towers and holy wells,
    That were part of the days that are gone.

And the friends—alas ! how few—
In the hours of anguish true,
Whose inmost hearts I knew,
    In the fire of the days that are gone.

And the dreams that once I dreamed
Of a nation's soul redeemed
From the hell in which she seemed
    A saint in the days that are gone

Still the tomb, the rath, the shrine,
And love's memories divine,
O rich in tears! are thine,
    Widowed queen of the days that are gone.

Sad isle of chains and graves,
Though thy sons are slaves of slaves,
I bless thee o'er the waves,
    For the sake of the days that are gone.

Thus memory like a breeze
Through the strong and silent trees,
Bows my manhood, strewing these
    Withered leaves of the days that are gone.

RICHARD D'ALTON WILLIAMS.

IN MEMORY OF RICHARD D'ALTON WILLIAMS.

THE early mower, heart-deep in the corn,
  Falls suddenly, to rise on earth no more;
The lark he startled carols to the morn,
  The field flowers blossom brightly as before,
Gay laughs the milk-maid to the shouting swain,
Who calls the dead afar, but calls in vain.

Thus in the world's wide harvest-field doth life,
  Unconscious of the stricken heart, rejoice;
Thus, through the city's thousand tones of strife,
  The true friend misses but the single voice;
Thus, while the tale of death fills every mouth,
For us there is but one—fallen in the South.

One that, amid far other scenes and years,
  Leal memory still recals full to our view,
Ere life as yet had reached the time of tears.
  When many hopes were garnered in a few—
Blithe was his jest in those fraternal days,
Before we reached the parting of the ways.

They were a band of brethren, richly graced
  With all that most exalts the sons of men—
Youth, courage, honour, conduct, wit well-placed—
  When shall we see their parallels again?
The very flower and fruitage of their age,
Destined for duty's cross or glory's page.

And he, our latest-lost among them all,
  No rival had for strangely-blended powers—
All shapes of beauty waited at his call :
  Soft Pity wept o'er Misery in showers,
Or honest Laughter, leaping from the heart,
Pealed her wild note beyond the reach of Art.

Meekly o'er all, the rare and priceless crown
  Of gentle, silent Pity he still wore—
Like some fair chapel in the midmost town,
  His busy heart was holy at the core ;
Deep there his virtues lay—no eye could trace
The Pharisee's prospectus in his face.

Sleep well, O Bard! too early from the field
  Of labour and of honour called away ;
Sleep, like a hero on your own good shield,
  Beneath the Shamrock wreathed about the bay.
Not doubtful is thy place among the host
Whom fame and Erin love and mourn the most.

THOMAS D'ARCY McGEE.

GOD BLESS THE BRAVE !

[The touching incident which inspired this poem requires to
be narrated in order that the lines may be understood.   During
the American war, two companies of Irish-American soldiers
happening to halt for a few days (between two battles) at Thibo-
deaux, Louisiana, where Richard D'Alton Williams had, shortly
before, breathed his last, saw his grave there, unmarked by stone
or inscription.   One of their captains was commissioned to go to
New Orleans, and with a fund raised among themselves to pur-
chase a monument which was reverently placed over the remains
of the dead poet before they marched away, with the following
inscription :—

Sacred to the Memory of
RICHARD D'ALTON WILLIAMS,
The Irish Patriot and Poet,
Who died July 5th, 1862. Aged 40 years.
This stone was erected by his countrymen serving in
Companies C and K, 8th Regt., N. H. Volunteers,
As a slight testimonial of their esteem
For his unsullied patriotism and his exalted devotion
To the cause of Irish Freedom.]

GOD bless the brave! the brave alone
  Were worthy to have done the deed.
A soldier's hand has raised the stone,
  Another traced the lines men read,
Another set the guardian rail
Above thy minstrel—Innisfail!

A thousand years ago—ah! then
  Had such a harp in Erin ceased
His cairn had met the eyes of men
  By every passing hand increased.

God bless the brave! not yet the race
Could coldly pass his dwelling place

Let it be told to old and young,
　At home, abroad, at fire, at fair,
Let it be written, spoken, sung,
　Let it be sculptured, pictured fair,
How the young braves stood weeping round
Their exiled poet's ransomed mound.

How lowly knelt and humbly prayed
　The lion-hearted brother band
Around the monument they made
　For him who sang the Fatherland!
A scene of scenes, where glory's shed
Both on the living and the dead.

THOMAS D'ARCY McGEE.

THE GOOD SHIP CASTLE DOWN.

(A REBEL CHAUNT, A.D. 1776.)

OH, how she plough'd the ocean, the good ship
    Castle Down,
That day we hung our colours out, the Harp without
    the Crown !
A gallant barque, she topp'd the wave, and fearless
    hearts were we,
With guns and pikes and bayonets, a stalwart
    company.
'Twas a sixteen years from THUROT; and sweeping
    down the bay
The "Siege of Carrickfergus" so merrily we did play :
And by the old castle's foot we went, with three
    right hearty cheers,
And wav'd aloft our green cockades, for we were
    Volunteers,

                        Volunteers !
Oh we were in our prime that day, stout Irish
    Volunteers.

'Twas when we heav'd our anchor on the breast of
    smooth Garmoyle,
Our guns spoke out in thunder : "Adieu, sweet Irish
    soil !"
At Whiteabbey and Greencastle, and Holywood so gay
Were hundreds waving handkerchiefs and many a
    loud huzza.

Our voices o'er the water struck the hollow mountains
    round—
Young Freedom, struggling at her birth, might utter
    such a sound.
By that green slope beside Belfast, we cheer'd and
    cheer'd it still—
For they had chang'd its name that year, and they
    call'd it Bunker's Hill.
                            Bunker's Hill !
Oh, were our hands but with our hearts in the trench
    at Bunker's Hill.

Our ship clear'd out for Quebec; but thither little
    bent,
Up some New England river, to run her keel we meant ;
So we took a course due north as round the old
    Black Head we steer'd,
Till Ireland bore south-west by south, and Fingal's
    rock appear'd.
Then on the poop stood Webster, while the ship
    hung flutteringly,
About to take her tack across the wide, wide ocean
    sea—
He pointed to th' Atlantic : "Sure yon's no place
    for slaves :
Haul down these British badges, for Freedom rules
    the waves,—
                    Rules the waves "—
Three hundred strong men answered, shouting
    "Freedom rules the Waves !"

Then all together rose and brought the British
    ensign down,
And up we haul'd our Irish green, without the
    British crown.
Emblazoned there a golden harp like a maiden
    undefiled,
A shamrock wreath around her head, look'd o'er the
    sea and smiled.
A hundred days, with adverse wind, we kept our
    course afar,
On the hundredth day came bearing down, a British
    sloop of war.
When they spied our flag they fired a gun, but as
    they near'd us fast,
Old Andrew Jackson went aloft and nailed it to
    the mast,—
                    To the mast!
A soldier was old Jackson and he made our colours
    fast.

Patrick Henry was our captain, as brave as ever
    sailed;
"Now we must do or die," said he, "for the green
    flag is nailed."
Silently came the sloop along; and silently we lay
Flat, till with cheers and loud broadside the foe
    began the fray:
Then the boarders o'er the bulwarks, like shuttlecocks,
    we cast;—
One close discharge from all our guns cut down
    the tapering mast:

"Now, British tars! St. George's Cross is trailing
    in the sea—
How d'ye like the greeting and the handsel of the
    Free?—
                         Of the Free!
How like you, lads, the greeting of the men who
    will be free?"

They answer'd us with cannon, as befitted well their
    fame;
And to shoot away our Irish flag each gunner took
    his aim;
They ripp'd it up in ribbons, till it fluttered in the air
And riddled it with shot-holes, till no Golden Harp
    was there;
But through the ragged holes the sky did glance
    and gleam in light,
Just as the twinkling stars shine through God's
    unfurled flag at night.
With dropping fire we sang "Good night, and fare
    ye well, brave tars!"
Our captain looked aloft: "By heaven! the flag is
    Stripes and Stars,"
                         Stripes and Stars!
So into Boston port we sailed, beneath the Stripes
    and Stars.

JAMES McBURNEY.

RHYMES FOR THE LANDLORDED.

1. EVICTION.

LONG years their cabin stood
    Out on the moor;
More than one sorrow-brood
    Passed through their door;
Ruin them over-cast,
Worse than the wintry blast;
Famine's plague followed fast:
    God help the poor!

Dying, or living here—
    Which is the worse?
Misery's heavy tear,
    Back to thy source!
Who dares to lift her head
Up from the scarcely dead?
Who pulls the crazy shed
    Down on the corse?

What though some rent was due,
    Hast thou no grace?
So may God pardon you,
    Shame of your race!
What though that home may be
Wretched and foul to see—
What if God harry thee
    Forth from His face?

2. REVENGE.

THE leaves are still ; not a breath is heard ;
  How bright the harvest day !
'Tis the tramp of a horse ; the boughs are stirred :
  The agent comes this way.
Was it an old gun-muzzle peeped
  Behind yon crimson leaf ?
  A shot !—and murder's bloody sheaf
          Is reaped.

Who sold the farm above his head ?
  Who drove the widow mad ?
Who pulled her dying from her bed ?
  Who robbed the idiot lad ?
Who sent the starved girl to the streets ?
  Who mocked grey Sorrow's smart ?
  Yes ! listen in thy blood !—His heart
          Yet beats.

Not one has help for the dying man ;
  Not one the murderer stays ;
Tho' all must see him where he ran,
  Not even the child betrays.
O Wrong !—thou hast a fearful brood !
  What inquest can ye need
  Who know Revenge but reaped the seed
          Of Blood ?

3. EMIGRATION.

STOOPS the sun behind the ocean;
   Darker shadows hide the bay;
And the last weak words are spoken,
From heart-breaking to heart-broken,
   As the ship gets under weigh.
Now the yellow moon is waning
   On the dim and lessening strand;
Darkly speeds *the Exile*, draining
   The life-blood of the Land.

Reck not Youth's intense emotion—
   Weeping Love, or white-brow'd Care,
Look on Manhood, spirit-broken;
On the dark signs that betoken
   Progress of the plague,—Despair.
Hopeless are the dim eyes, straining
   Tow'rd that woe-worn pilgrim band:
Darkly speeds *the Exile*, draining
   The life-blood of the Land.

WILLIAM JAMES LINTON.

COME, LIBERTY, COME!

COME, Liberty, come! we are ripe for thy coming;
    Come, freshen the hearts where thy rival has trod;
Come, richest and rarest! come, purest and fairest!
    Come, daughter of science! come, gift of the god!

Long, long have we sighed for thee, coyest of maidens!
    Long, long have we worshipped thee, queen of
        the brave!
 Steadily sought for thee, readily fought for thee,
    Purpled the scaffold and glutted the grave!

Still in the ranks are we, struggling with eagerness,
    Still in the battle for Freedom are we!
Words may avail in it, swords if they fail in it,
    What matters the weapon if only we're free?

Oh, we are pledged in the face of the universe,
    Never to falter and never to swerve;
Toil for it! bleed for it! if there be need for it—
    Stretch every sinew and strain every nerve.

Irishmen! Irishmen! think what is Liberty,
    Fountain of all that is valued and dear;
Peace and security, knowledge and purity,
    Hope for hereafter, and happiness here.

H

Nourish it, treasure it deep in your inner heart,
  Think of it ever by night and by day;
Pray for it! sigh for it! work for it! die for it!
  What is this life and dear freedom away?

List! scarce a sound can be heard in our thorough-
    fares;
  Look! scarce a ship can be seen on our streams;
Heart-crushed and desolate, spell-bound, irresolute,
  Ireland but lives in the by-gone of dreams.

Irishmen! if we be true to our promises,
  Nerving our souls for more fortunate hours,
Life's choicest blessings, love's fond caressings,
  Peace, home, and happiness—all shall be ours!

DENIS FLORENCE MACCARTHY.

MY OWN SWEET RIVER LEE.

My own dear native river, how fondly dost thou flow
By many a fair and sunny scene where I can never go.
Thy waves are free to wander, and quickly on they wind,
Till thou hast left the crowded streets and city
    far behind;
Beyond, I may not follow, thy haunts are not for me;
Yet I love to think on the pleasant track of my
    own sweet river Lee!

The springtide now is breaking, where thy waters
    glance along
Full many a herd salutes thee with bright and
    cheering song,
Full many a sunbeam falleth upon thy bosom fair,
And every nook thou seekest hath welcome smiling
    there.
Glide on, thou blessed river! nor pause to think of me
Who, only in my longing heart, can tread that
    track with thee!

Yet, when thy waters wander, where haughty in decay,
Some grand old Irish castle looks frowning on thy
    way—
Oh, speak aloud, bold river! how I have wept
    with pride
To read of those past ages, ere all our glory died;

And wish for one short moment I had been there
 to see
Such relic of the bygone day upon thy banks, fair Lee !

And if, in roving onward, thy gladsome waters bound
Where cottage homes are smiling and children's
 voices sound,
Oh, think how sweet and tranquil, beneath the
 loving sky—
Rejoicing in some country home, my life had glided
 by,
And grieve one little moment that I can never be
A happy cottage maiden upon thy banks, fair Lee !

Now, fare thee well, glad river ! peace smile upon
 thy way,
And still may sunbeams brighten where thy wild
 rimples play !
Oft, in that weary city thy blue waves leave behind,
I'll think upon the pleasant paths where thy smooth
 waters wind.
Oh, but for one long summer's day to wander on
 with thee
And rove where'er thou rovest, my own sweet river Lee!

ELLEN MARY DOWNING.

THE GOBBAN SAOR.

[In Petrie's "Round Towers" there is a short account of "The Gobban Saor"—their builder. He is there supposed to have lived in the first Christian age of Ireland, the 6th century; but his birth, life and death are involved in great obscurity and many legends. He is, perhaps, after Finn and St. Patrick, the most popular personage in the ancient period of Irish history.]

HE step'd a man, out on the ways of men,
    And no one knew his sept, or rank, or name;
Like a strong stream far issuing from a glen,
    From some source unexplored the Master came;
Gossips there were who, wondrous keen of ken,
    Surmised that he must be a child of shame;
Others declared him of the Druids, then—
    Thro' Patrick's labours—fall'n from power and fame.

He lived apart, wrapt up in many plans;
    He woo'd not women, tasted not of wine;
He shunn'd the sports and councils of the clans;
    Nor ever knelt at a frequented shrine.
His orisons were old poetic ranns
    Which the new Olamhs deem'd an evil sign;
To most he seem'd one of those Pagan Khans
    Whose mystic vigor knows no cold decline.

He was the builder of the wondrous Towers,
    Which, tall and straight and exquisitely round,
Rise monumental round this isle of ours,
    Index-like, marking spots of holy ground.

In gloaming silent glens, in lowland bowers,
   On river banks, these *Cloiteachs* old abound,
Where Art, enraptured, meditates long hours
   And Science ponders, wondering and spell-bound.

Lo, wheresoe'er these pillar-towers aspire,
   Heroes and holy men repose below;
The bones of some, gleaned from a Pagan pyre,
   Others in armour lie, as for a foe;
It was the mighty Master's life-desire
   To chronicle his great ancestors so;
What holier duty, what achievement higher
   Remains to us, than this he thus doth show?

Yet he, the builder, died an unknown death;
   His labours done, no man beheld him more;
'Twas thought his body faded like a breath—
   Or, like a sea-mist, floated off Life's shore.
Doubt overhangs his fate—and faith—and birth:
   His works alone attest his life and love,
They are the only witnesses he hath,
   All else Egyptian darkness covers o'er.

Men called him GOBBAN SAOR, and many a tale
   Yet lingers in the byways of the land,
Of how he cleft the rock, and down the vale
   Led the bright river, child-like, in his hand;

Of how on giant ships he spread great sail
  And many marvels else, by him first planned,
And tho' these legends fail, in Innisfail
  His name and Towers for centuries still shall stand

THOMAS D'ARCY McGEE.

MY PEERLESS BOY.

IN many a woe have I betaken,
  My gentle lyre, myself to thee.
And deemed my heart not all forsaken
  If still thy strings would speak to me;
But *then*, with thy consoling measure,
  Was blent an undertone of joy,
From one unmasked, one hidden pleasure—
  The presence of my Peerless Boy.

I loved him!—but till he lay sleeping
  With death's cold shadow on his brow
Ne'er seemed the treasure in my keeping
  So precious as I feel it now!
He lent to every hope and feeling
  A secret but pervading joy;
And thou, my lyre, wert only stealing
  Thy music from my Peerless Boy.

And shall my grief not be forgiven?
Though minstrel spirits be endued
To soar and sing, like birds to heaven,
  They must descend to earth for food:
And where shall I, whose soul was bounded
  To him, its sole sustaining joy,
Find comfort since the knell has sounded
  The requiem of my Peerless Boy?

Oh, sweet it was, past human telling,
  To see his young eye catching fire,
And watch his full heart proudly swelling
  Beneath the lessons of my lyre.
And, if there be an hour conferring
  On . mortal an immortal's joy,
I felt it when my song was stirring
  The spirit of my Peerless Boy.

No more shall element, or season,
  Or scene, assist me to impart
New truth and vigor to his reason—
  New grace and beauty to his heart.
We ne'er shall roam, as oft together,
  When even our silence had its joy:
He moulders in the grave, and thither
  I hasten to my Peerless Boy.

J. De J. Frazer.

TO DUFFY IN PRISON.

'Twas but last night I traversed the Atlantic's
 furrow'd face—
The stars but thinly colonized the wilderness of
 space—
A white sail glinted here and there, and sometimes
 o'er the swell,
Rang the seaman's song of labor or the silvery
 night-watch bell;
I dreamt I reached the Irish shore and felt my heart
 rebound
From wall to wall within my breast, as I trod that
 holy ground;
I sat down by my own hearth-stone, beside my
 love again—
I met my friends, and Him, the first of friends, and
 Irish men.

I saw once more the dome-like brow, the large and
 lustrous eyes;
I mark'd upon the sphinx-like face the cloud of
 thoughts arise,
I heard again that clear quick voice that as a trumpet
 thrill'd
The souls of men, and wielded them even as the
 speaker will'd—

I felt the cordial-clasping hand that never feigned
    regard,
Nor ever dealt a muffled blow, or nicely weighed
    reward.
My friend ! my friend!—oh, would to God that you
    were here with me—
A-watching in the starry west for Ireland's liberty !

Oh, Brothers, I can well declare, who read it like
    a scroll,
What Roman characters were stamp'd upon that
    Roman soul.
The courage, constancy and love—the old-time faith
    and truth—
The wisdom of the sages—the sincerity of youth—
Like an oak upon our native hills, a host might
    camp there-under,
Yet it bare the song-birds in its core, amid the
    storm and thunder ,
It was the gentlest, firmest soul that ever, lamp-like
    showed
A young race seeking freedom up her misty mountain
    road.

Like a convoy from the flag-ship' our fleet is scattered
    far,
And you, the valiant Admiral, chained and imprisoned
    are—

Like a royal galley's precious freight flung on sea-
sunder'd strands,

The diamond wit and golden worth are far-cast on
the lands,

And I, whom most you lov'd, am here, and I can
but indite

My yearnings and my heart hopes, and curse *them*
while I write,

Alas! alas! ah what are prayers, and what are moans
or sighs,

When the heroes of the land are lost—of the land
that will not RISE.

They will bring you in their manacles beneath their
blood-red rag,   .

They will chain you like the conqueror to some sea-
moated crag.

To their slaves it will be given your great spirit to
annoy,

To fling falsehood in your cup, and to break your
martyr joy,

But you will bear it nobly, as Regulus did of eld,

The oak will be the oak, and honored e'en when fell'd;

Change is brooding over earth, it will find you mid
the main,

And throned between its wings you'll reach your
native land again.

THOMAS D'ARCY McGEE.

NEW YORK, *October 25th*, 1848.

WAITING FOR THE MAY.

Ah ! my heart is weary waiting,
　　Waiting for the May—
Waiting for the pleasant rambles,
Where the fragrant hawthorn brambles,
　With the woodbine alternating,
　　Scent the dewy way.
　Ah ! my heart is weary waiting,
　　Waiting for the May.

Ah ! my heart is sick with longing,
　　Longing for the May—
Longing to escape from study,
To the young face fair and ruddy,
　And the thousand charms belonging
　　To the summer s day.
　Ah ! my heart is sick with longing,
　　Longing for the May.

Ah ! my heart is sore with sighing,
　　Sighing for the May—
Sighing for their sure returning,
When the summer beams are burning,
　Hopes and flowers that dead or dying
　　All the winter lay.
　Ah! my heart is sore with sighing,
　　Sighing for the May.

Ah ! my heart is pained with throbbing
    Throbbing for the May—
Throbbing for the sea-side billows,
Or the water-wooing willows ;
    Where in laughing and in sobbing
    Glide the streams away.
    Ah ! my heart, my heart is throbbing,
    Throbbing for the May.

Waiting sad, dejected, weary,
    Waiting for the May.
Spring goes by with wasted warnings,
Moonlit evenings, sunbright mornings ;
    Summer comes, yet dark and dreary
    Life still ebbs away :
    Man is ever weary, weary,
    Waiting for the May !

              Denis Florence MacCarthy.

THE POET'S EGERIA.

THERE came a dream of most divine delight
 To soothe my soul tossed in a wild unrest;
Two soft fair hands lay on my matted hair,
 And my brow throbbed upon a loving breast.

A form, methought, in youth's most glowing May—
 A form, in mould of heavenly contour cast—
A form, which shrined a high aspiring soul—
 Within my circling arms was prisoned fast.

And eyes which rule my life—as polar stars
 Above the trusting seaman soar and shine—
Dear eyes, fond eyes, eyes of benignant light,
 Looked with a loving kindness into mine;

From a high brow where one might fitly set
 The antique crown of some heroic race;
A proud fair brow; but made divinely sweet
 When smiles lit up earth's loveliest human face.

And that fair type of perfect womankind,
 Methought did love me with ingenuous truth;
And gave to me, unworthy of such grace,
 Her woman's faith, her warm and lovely youth

Fame, friendship, gain—whatever move men's souls—
  Are ice-cold all, after that dream of bliss;
I walk alone amid the jostling crowd,
  Rapt in the memory of her parting kiss.

Matchless Egeria! vision of delight!
  Which on my drear and dungeoned life did
    break,
As blessed sunshine beams through prison bars;
  Oh, dream divine! why did I ever wake?

CHARLES GAVAN DUFFY.

O'CLERY'S PROPHESY.

A.D. 1600.

[Hugh O'Neill had a poet, O'Clery, who foretold the victory
of the Blackwater.   The original of the following lines may have
been written by the same hand, as I first met with them in an
old MS. in the Burgundian Library at Brussels, among other
fragments left by Friar Michael O'Clery, the chief of the "Four
Masters."—Author's Note.]

By the Druid's stone I slept,
While my dog his vigil kept,
And there on the mountain lone,
By that old weird-raising stone,
Visions wrapt me round, and voices
Spoke the word my soul rejoices.

"Bard ! the stranger's roof shall fall.
Grass shall grow in Norman hall,
Mileadh's race shall rise again,
Lords of mountain and of glen ;
Nial's blood, and Brian's seed—
Known for kingly word and deed—
Ollamh's skill and Ogma's lore
Time to Banbha will restore.

"Destiny has doomed it so !
Through pass of death, and waves of woe,
Banbha's sons shall come and go ;

Twelve score years a foreign brood
Shall warm them in the native blood—
Shall lord it in the fields of Eri,
Till her sons of life are weary.

"When the long-wronged men of Eri
Of their very lives are weary,
In that hour from cave and rath
Mighty souls shall find a path—
They who won in Gaul dominion;
They who cut the Eagle's pinion;
They of the prophetic race,
They of the fierce blood of Thrace,
They who Man and Mona lorded *
Shall regain the land and guard it "

So, upon that mountain lone,
By the grey weird-raising stone,
Visions wrapped me round and voices
Spake the word my soul rejoices.

THOMAS D'ARCY McGEE

* The Picts are derived by ancient tradition from Thrace.
Besides their Scottish colony the Irish had dominion over the
Isles of Man and Mona (Anglesey).

THE FAMINE YEAR.

WEARY men what reap ye?—"Golden corn for the
    stranger."
What sow ye?—"Human corses that await for the
    Avenger."
Fainting forms, all hunger-stricken, what see you in
    the offing?
"Stately ships to bear our food away, amid the
    stranger's scoffing."
There's a proud array of soldiers—what do they round
    your door?
"They guard our master's granaries from the thin
    hands of the poor."
Pale mothers, wherefore weeping?—"Would to God
    that we were dead—
"Our children swoon before us, and we cannot give
    them bread!'

Little children, tears are strange upon your infant
    faces,
God meant you but to smile within your mother's
    soft embraces.
"Oh, we know not what is smiling, and we know
    not what is dying;
"But we're hungry, very hungry, and we cannot stop
    our crying;

"And some of us grow cold and white—we know
    not what it means.
"But as they lie beside us, we tremble in our dreams."
There's a gaunt crowd on the highway—are ye come
    to pray to man,
With hollow eyes that cannot weep, and for words
    your faces wan?

"No; the blood is dead within our veins, we care
    not now for life;
"Let us die hid in the ditches, far from children and
    from wife;
"We cannot stay to listen to their ravings, famished
    cries—
"Bread! Bread! Bread!—and none to still their
    agonies.
"We left an infant playing with her dead mother's
    hand:
"We left a maiden maddened by the fever's scorching
    brand:
"Better, maiden, thou wert strangled in thy own
    dark-twisted tresses!
"Better, infant, thou wert smothered in thy mother's
    first caresses.

"We are fainting in our misery, but God will hear
    our groan;
"Yea, if fellow-men desert us, He will hearken from
    His throne!

" Accursed are we in our own land, yet toil we still
    and toil ;
" But the stranger reaps our harvest—the alien owns
    our soil.
" O Christ, how have we sinned, that on our native
    plains
" We perish houseless, naked, starved, with branded
    brow, like Cain's ?
" Dying, dying wearily, with a torture sure and
    slow—
" Dying as a dog would die, by the wayside as we
    go.

" One by one they're falling round us, their pale
    faces to the sky ;
" We've no strength left to dig them graves—
    there let them lie.
" The wild bird, when he's stricken, is mournèd
    by the others,
" But we, we die in Christian land—we die amid
    our brothers—
" In the land which God has given—like a wild beast
    in his cave,
" Without a tear, a prayer, a shroud, a coffin, or a
    grave.
" Ha ! but think ye the contortions on each dead
    face ye see,
" Shall not be read on judgment-day by the
    eyes of Deity ?

"We are wretches, famished, scorned, human tools
    to build your pride,
"But God will yet take vengeance for the souls
    for whom Christ died.
"Now is your hour of pleasure, bask ye in the
    world's caress;
"But our whitening bones against ye will arise as
    witnesses,
"From the cabins and the ditches, in their charred,
    uncoffined masses,
"For the ANGEL OF THE TRUMPET will know them
    as he passes.
"A ghastly, spectral army before great God we'll
    stand
"And arraign ye as our murderers, O spoilers of
    our land!"

SPERANZA (LADY WILDE).

"NO IRISH NEED APPLY."

[It would appear that this rejoinder was provoked by an advertisement (not uncommon at the time it was written 1845 in the Dublin papers) for an English or foreign servant, with the proviso which forms the refrain of this *jeu d'esprit:* what lent the exclusion additional piquancy was the fact which had become known, that the advertiser was an Englishman employed in Ireland, at a very high salary, as a Poor Law Commissioner.]

THANK you, John Bull, for this nice little summary—
Here is no "message of peace" and such flummery—
    Here, you would scorn to bamboozle or lie—
Stript of its metaphors, shorn of its mystery,
Here is our share of your statute-book's history—
    "For Justice and Right, let no Irish apply!"
        Hear it, oh, Irishmen,
        Boorish or squirishmen,
    Whether your station be low or be high—
        From wigged men to watchmen,
        English and Scotch men
    Are the fittest to trust, so you need not apply!

Every spring "the Great Talk" is commenced at
    St. Stephen's,
The sweet lips of Royalty soothe every grievance,
    And Chartists may threaten, and Welshmen
    defy!

But lest Justice should hitherward wander, to spancel
  her,
England proclaims through her learned Lord Chan.
  cellor,
     "The Irish are aliens,"* so needn't apply!
        Hear it, oh, Irishman,
        Peasant or squirishman,
     With a flush on your cheek, and a flash in
        your eye—
        Milesians! Cromwellians!
        Ye're nothing but aliens
     In language and race, so you needn't apply.

Suppose Mr. Rothschild would take into partnership
A poor struggling merchant who had neither chart
  nor ship,
     Would Roth. live in a palace—the "Co."
        in a sty?
Vould he take all his labour, his time, and his talents,
And say, when the latter applied for his balance,
     "You're an Irishman, Pat, so you needn't apply?"
        Well, gallant Irishman,
        Peasant or squirishman,
     This you are told, and you pause to reply?
        England says *this* to you!
        Have you no fist to you?
     Signs are sometimes the best way to reply.

* It was Lord Lyndhurst who used this memorable expression.

Well! the meaning of one little line is surprising—
We have spoken and met, what is left?—advertising!
Some notice like this 'tis no harm if we try :—
WANTED FOR IRELAND a true native Parliament,
Better than that won by Grattan and Charlemont—
NOTA BENE: *"No English or Scotch need apply!"*
This is *our* ultimatum,
We don't love or don't hate 'en,
But the wants of our island her sons can
supply—
Boorish or squirishmen,
They *must* be Irishmen—
So Johnny and Sawney, you needn't apply

DENIS FLORENCE MACCARTHY.

THE RETURN.

At length beneath the roof we rest
　That sheltered us when life was young,
In this old window tow'rds the West,
　Where oft in twilight's glow we've sung;
Still bright the mountain's starry rim,
　Still fresh the trees around the door;
But where are they, the lost, the dim,
　Whose forms shall light it never more?

Ah me! how many an afternoon,
　Along yon ivied lane we went—
The low wind breathing from the moon—
　The dead leaves wafting wintry scent;
The ruin gloomed the holy ground,
　The fields were full of fading light—
The beat of barrack drums was round—
　The dead West rolling tow'rd the night.

Rememberest thou old summer time
　When, the long studious day now o'er,
Entranc'd we sat in talk sublime
　Drawn from some storied page of yore?
Rich fancies, themes abstruse, old songs,
　From varied lips were heard to rise—
Ah! where are those old spirit throngs
　Long passed beyond yon crimson skies?

Perchance with silent eyes to-night
   They gaze upon us from afar ;
Perchance their dreams from spheres of light
   Float tow'rd us on this green old star ;
And each old friend, each long-lost hour,
   Each field and brook and song they knew
Strikes o'er their memory with the power
   That strews these tears between us two.

The low wind moans along the hill,
   The ivy round the casement shakes,
The full moon rises slow and still
   And drifts the fields with silver flakes :—
Then let us o'er this shadow'd bowl
   Clasp these old hands, and while the breath
Flows through us, charm the silent soul
   With dreams of vanish'd joy—and death.

                       ANONYMOUS.

SHE'S COME! SHE'S COME!

SHE'S come! She's come!
I wondered at first why a tenderer light
Added beauty to day, and new lustre to night;
And I wondered to see a fresh bloom on the flowers,
And the laughter and joy that came on with the hours:
The skies they are brighter, the breezes are lighter,
The rivers are fleeter, all music is sweeter,
And earth seems refreshed and endued with new powers!
While the secret of all, though no secret to some,
Is the sight of the Loved One—She's come! She's come!

She's come! She's come!
I wondered at first at such glory and gladness;
For earth has no shadows, and men have no sadness:
Care, grief, and misfortune, from mortals have flown;
And Nature is proud as a queen on her throne;
The breezes, the vagrants, go round with *her* fragrance,
And the pinks and sweet briars are robbers and liars,
For 'tis *her* breath they've stolen, ashamed of their own;
While the secret of all, though no secret to some,
To the presence of Ellen—She's come! She's come!

She's come! She's come!
'Tis surprising how brilliantly all things are glancing!
The business of life now's but singing and dancing.
No wonder 'tis Jubilee! Lord, it begins—
And all the wide world will be pardoned their sins!

Methinks I could fly now, my spirit's so high now—
But, stop—is it plain, man, that I'm not insane, man,
Yet, granting I'm mad as the maddest O'Flynns,*
Still the secret of all, though no secret to some,
Is the sight of the dear one—She's come ! She's come !

She's come ! She's come !
Go tell the old sun, whom our bards sing the praise of,
To take a short rest, let him now lay his rays off !
And the moon—put it to her old age to say whether
They might not enjoy a vacation together :
We don't want their light now, by day or by night now,
And the stars needn't cluster—we've two with more lustre
Than all that the firmament gives altogether !
Whilst the secret of all, though no secret to some,
Is the light of the Loved One—She's come ! She's come !

ANONYMOUS.

* There liveth a family in this quarter, named O'Flynne, of
which report hath it that few of them be *compos mentis* in ordinary
matters.—SPENSER'S " Case of Ireland Stated."

THE REASON.

[Some verses having appeared in the *Nation* complaining of the long silence of the writer of this ballad, the following is the answer :—" One of the most tender and touching," the editor of the *Nation* wrote at the time, " he had ever read, and the more so that the death of a dear child gives it a force beyond the reach of art."]

My spirit o'er an early tomb,
  With ruffled wing, sits drooping ;
And real forms of blighted bloom
Have in my heart left little room
  For forms of fancy's grouping.
The heart, the eye, I loved to light
  With song, are dark and hollow ;
Ah, if, when the young eye was bright,
I took a haughty minstrel flight,
It was to tempt the inborn might
  Of that young heart to follow !

No more—ah, never more, his gaze
  Shall be to me as glory !
No more—ah, never more, my lays
Shall sway him with a hope to raise
  His country, and her story !
And when the loved ones in the numb
  Deaf trance of death are wreathèd
(Though sweet may be his song to some)

The singer feels the hour is come
For lyre and lyrist to be dumb—
  His best of song is breathèd.

'Tis true it was a joy to see
  The slave for freedom wrestle,
Stirr'd by my random minstrelsy;
But 'tis not in the lofty tree
  The sweetest song birds nestle:
They are a shy and chary race—
  And though they soar and squander
Rich music over nature's face,
To one deep, lonely dwelling-place
No foot may find, no eye may trace,
  They still return the fonder.

Oh, God!—But prayers availed me not!
  The darkening angel entered,
And made one universal blot—
A world-wide desert of the spot
  Where all my hope was centered!
The heart, the eye, I loved to light
  With song, are dark and hollow:
What marvel, if my spirit slight
The guerdon of the minstrel's flight?
I cannot tempt the inborn might
  Of that young heart to follow.

J. De Jean Frazer.

1.

THE VOICE OF THE POOR.

WAS sorrow ever like unto our sorrow?
  Oh, God above!
Will our night never change into a morrow
  Of joy and love?
A deadly gloom is on us—waking—sleeping—
  Like the darkness at noon-tide
That fell upon the pallid Mother, weeping
  By the Crucified.

Before us die our brothers of starvation:
  Around are cries of famine and despair:
Where is hope for us, or comfort, or salvation?
  Where, oh, where?
If the angels ever hearken, downward bending,
  They are weeping, we are sure,
At the litanies of human groans, ascending
  From the crushed hearts of the poor.

When the human rests in love upon the human,
  All grief is light;
But who bends one kind glance to illumine
  Our life-long night?
The air around is ringing with their laughter.
  God has only made the rich to smile:
And we, in our rags and want and woe, we follow after,
  Weeping the while.

And the laughter seems but utter'd to deride us—
    When, oh! when,
Will fall the frozen barriers that divide us
    From other men?
Will ignorance for ever thus enslave us!
    Will misery for ever lay us low?
All are eager with their insults, but to save us
    None, none we know.

We never knew a childhood's mirth and gladness
    Nor the proud heart of youth, free and brave;
Oh! a death-like dream of wretchedness and sadness
    Is our life's weary journey to the grave.
Day by day we lower sink and lower,
    Till the God-like soul within
Falls crushed, beneath the fearful demon power
    Of poverty and sin.

So we toil on—on, with fever burning
    In heart and brain;
So we toil on—on, thro' bitter scorning—
    Want, woe and pain:
We dare not raise our eyes to the blue heaven
    Or the toil must cease—
We dare not breathe the fresh air God has given,
    One hour in peace.

We must toil, though the light of life is burning,
  Oh, how dim!
We must toil on our sick bed, feebly turning
  Our eyes to Him
Who alone can hear the pale lip faintly saying
  With scarce moved breath,—
And the paler hands, uplifted, and the praying,—
  "Lord, grant us *Death!*"

SPERANZA (LADY WILDE).

WORK WHILE IT IS CALLED DAY.

"No man hath hired us"—strong hands drooping
  Listless falling in idleness down;
Men in the silent market place grouping
  Round Christ's cross of silent stone.
"No man hath hired us"—pale hands pining,
  Stalwart forms bowed down to sue—
"The red dawn is passed, noon is shining,
  But no man hath given us work to do."

Then a Voice seemed to peal from the heights of
    heaven :—
  "Men," it said, "of the Irish soil!
"I gave ye a land as a Garden of Eden,
  "Where you and your sons should till and toil;
K

"I set your throne by the glorious waters,
  "Where ocean flung round you her mighty
    bands,
"That your sails, like those of your Tyrian
    fathers,
  "Might sweep the shores of a hundred lands.

"Power I gave to the hands of your leaders
  "Wisdom I gave to the lips of the wise,
"And your children grew as the stately cedars
  "That shadow the streams of Paradise.
"What have ye done with my land of beauty?
  "Has the spoiler bereft her of robe and crown?
"Have my people failed in a people's duty?
  "Has the wild boar trampled my vineyard down?"

"True," they answered, faint in replying,
  "Our vines are rent by the wild boar's tusks;
"The corn on our golden slopes is lying,
  "But our children feed on the remnant husks.
"Our strong men lavish their blood for others;
  "Our prophets and wise men are heard no more;
"Our young men give a kiss to their mothers,
  "Then sail away for a foreign shore."

Then the Lord came down from the heights of
    heaven,
  Came down to that garden fair to view,
Where the weary men waited, from morn' till even,
  For some one to give them work to do.

"Ye have sinned," He said, and the angel lustre
  Darkened slowly as bright clouds may ;
"Weeds are growing where fruit should cluster—
  "Yet ye stand idle all the day."

"Have ye trod in the furrows, and worked as
    truly
  "As men who knew they reap as they sow?
"Have ye flung in the seed and watched it duly,
  "Day and night, lest the tares should grow?
"Have ye tended the vine my hand hath planted?
  "Pruned and guided its tendrils fair,
"Ready with all things that might be wanted
  "To strengthen the fruit its branches bear?

"Who knoweth the time of the new dispensations ;
  "Go on in faith, and the light will come ;
"The last may yet be first amongst nations ;
  "Wait till the end for the final doom."
The last may be first ! Shall our country's glory
  Ever flash light on the path we have trod?
Who knows ? Who knows? for our future story
  Lies hid in the great sealed Book of God.

LADY WILDE.

WORDS OF FOREWARNING.

YOUTHS! Compatriots! Friends! Men for the time
    that is nearing!
Spirits appointed by Heaven to front the storm and
    the trouble!
You, who in seasons of peril, unfaltering still and
    unfearing,
Calmly have held on your course, the course of the
    Just and the Noble!
YOU, young men, would a man unworthy to rank
    in your number,
Yet with a heart that bleeds for his country's wrongs
    and affliction,
Fain raise a voice to, in song, albeit his music and
    diction
Rather be fitted, alas, to lull to, than startle from,
    slumber.

FRIENDS! the gloom in our land, in our once bright
    land, grows deeper.
Suffering, even to death, in its horriblest forms,
    aboundeth ;
Thro' our black harvestless fields, the peasants' faint
    wail resoundeth.
Hark to it, even now! . . The night-mare oppressèd
    sleeper

Gasping and struggling for life, beneath his hideous
    bestrider,   .
Sëeth not, drëcth not, sight or terror more fearful
    or ghastly
Than that poor paralysed slave! Want, House-
    lessness, Famine, and lastly
Death in a thousand-corpsed grave, that momently
    waxeth wider.

WORSE! The great heart of the country is thrilled
    and throbbeth but faintly!
Apathy palsieth *here*—and *there*, a panic misgiving:
Even the Trustful and Firm, even the Sage and the
    Saintly,
Seem to believe that the Dead but foreshow the
    doom of the Living.
Men of the faithfullest souls all but broken hearted
O'er the dishonoured tombs of the glorious dreams,
    that have perished—
Dreams that almost outshone Realities while they
    were cherished—
All, they exclaim, is gone! The Vision and Hope
    have departed!

WORST AND SADDEST. As, under Milton's lower-
    most Tophet
Yawned another yet lower, so for the mourning Million
Still is there deeper woe! Patriot, Orator, Prophet,
Some who a few years agone stood proudly in the
    Pavilion   ·

Of their land's rights and liberties, gazing abroad
  thro' its casement
On the fair Future they fondly deemed at hand
  for their nation,
Now not alone succumb to the Change and the
  Degradation,
But have ceased even to feel them! God! *this*
  indeed is abasement!

IS THE LAST HOPE THEN GONE? Must we lie down
  despairing?
No! there is always hope for all who will dare
  and suffer;
Hope for all who surmount the Hill of Exertion,
  uncaring
Whether their path be brighter or darker, smoother
  or rougher;
No! there is always hope for those who, relying
  with earnest
Souls on God and themselves take for their
  motto, 'Labour.'
Such see the rainbow's glory where Heaven looms
  darkest and sternest:
Such in the storm-wind hear but the music of pipe
  and tabor.

FOLLOW YOUR DESTINY UP! Work! Write! Preach
  to arouse and
Warn, and watch and encourage! Dangers, no
  doubt, surround you—

But for Ten threatening you now, you will soon be
appalled by a Thousand
If you forsake the course to which Virtue and Honour
have bound you !
Oh, persevere ! persevere ! Falter not !—faint not !—
shrink not !
Hate and Hostility serve but as spurs to the will
of the Zealous—
Tho' your foes flourish awhile, and you *seem* to
decline, be not jealous,
" Help from the Son of Man cometh in such an
hour as you think not !"

SLAVERY DEBASES THE SOUL, yea! reverses its primal
nature ;
Long were our fathers bowed to the earth with
fetters of iron—
And alas ! we inherit the failings and ills that environ
Slaves like a dungeon wall and dwarf their original
stature.
Look on your countrymen's failings with less of
anger than pity ;
Even with the faults of the evil deal in a manner
half tender ;
And like an army encamped before a beleagured
city,
Earlier or later you must compel your foes to
surrender !

Lo, A NEW YEAR ! A year, into whose bosom Time
    gathers
All the past lessons of ages—a mournful but truth-
    teaching muster ;
All the rich thoughts and deeds and the marvellous
    lore of our fathers ;   ,
All the sunlike experience that makes men wiser
    and juster.
Hail it with steadfast resolve — thankfully, if it
    befriend you—
Guardedly, lest it betray—without either Despair
    or Elation,
Panoplied inly against the sharpest ills it may send you,
But with a high hope still for yourselves and the
    Rise of your Nation.

OMEN FULL, archèd with gloom and laden with
    many a presage,
Many a portent of woe, looms the Impending Era,
Not as of old, by comet, sword, Gorgon, or ghastly
    Chimera,
Scarcely by lightning and thunder, Heaven to-day
    sends its message
Into the secret heart—down thro' the caves of the
    spirit,
Pierces the silent shaft—sinks the invisible token—
Cloaked in the Hall, the Envoy stands, his mission
    unspoken,
While the pale banquetless guests await in trembling
    to hear it.

                JAMES CLARENCE MANGAN.

THE FOUR MASTERS.

[The great historical record, known in Irish as "Annala rioghachta Eireann" and in English as the "Annals of the Kingdom of Ireland, by the Four Masters," is certainly the most valuable title deed of Ireland's nationality. Its *Index Nominum* supplies a roll of many thousands of the notable men and women who lived in Ireland from the time of St. Patrick to the year of our Lord 1616—her kings and chiefs, her warriors and sages, her poets and her priests. Its *Index Locorum* indicates, by their true names, many thousands of places which have been the scenes of memorable events in Irish history. Of the "Four Masters" who compiled this priceless summary, Michael O'Clery, "a poor brother of the order of St. Francis," was the principal. Before entering on his labour of love, O'Clery spent ten years in travelling about the country, collecting MSS. and materials from the religious houses and elsewhere. The munificence of Feargal Lord O'Gara and the hospitality of the brethren of the Franciscan convent of Donegal enabled Brother Michael and his colleagues to work uninterruptedly at their compilation for five years—*i.e.*, from 1632 to 1636. When it was finished O'Clery dedicated it to his patron Lord O'Gara, and left it in his hands, returning himself to his friary at Louvain, where he died in 1643. McGee appears to have cherished a singular affection for Brother Michael O'Clery. He has written many poems in honour of him; and in his earliest work, "The Irish Writers of the 17th Century," there is an interesting memoir of O'Clery and his associates. —ED.]

MANY altars are in Banva,
Many chancels hung in white,
Many schools and many abbeys
Glorious in our fathers' sight;

Yet whene'er I go a pilgrim
   Back, dear Native Isle, to thee,
May my filial footsteps bear me
   To that Abbey by the sea—
To that Abbey—roofless, doorless,
   Shrineless, monkless, though it be!

These are days of swift up-building;
   All to pride and triumph tends;
Art is liegeman to Religion;—
   Wealth on Genius now attends.
As the day-beam to the sailor,
   Lighting up the wrecker's shore—
So the present lustre shineth
   And our dangers all are o'er—
But no gleam rests on that Abbey,
   Silent by Tyrconnel's shore.

Yet I hear them in my musings,
   And I see them as I gaze,—
Four meek men around the cresset,
   Reading scrolls of other days;
Four unwearied scribes who treasure
   Every word and every line—
Saving every ancient sentence
   As if writ by hands divine.

On their calm down-bended foreheads
  Tell me what it is you read?
Is there malice, or ambition,
  Selfish will, or selfish deed?
Oh, no, no! the angel Duty
  Sheds his light within these walls;
And their four worn right hands follow
  Where the Angel's radiance falls.

Not of fame, and not of fortune,
  Do these eager pensmen dream;
Darkness shrouds the hills of Banva,
  Sorrow sits by every stream;
One by one the lights that led her,
  Hour by hour, are quenched in gloom;
But the patient, sad, Four Masters,
  Toil on in their lonely room—
  Duty still defying Doom.

As the breathing of the west wind
  Over bound and bearded sheaves—
As the murmur in the bee-hives
  Softly heard on summer eves—
So the rustle of the vellum,—
  So the anxious voices, sound;—
While a deep expectant silence
  Seems to listen all around.

Brightly on the Abbey gable
　Shines the full moon thro' the night,
While afar to northward glances
　All the bay in waves of light:
Tufted isle,·and splinter'd headland
　Smile and soften in her ray;
Yet within their dusky chamber
　The meek Masters toil alway,
　Finding all too short the day.

Now they kneel! oh, list the accents,
　From the souls of mourners wrung;
Hear the soaring aspirations
　In the old ancestral tongue;
For the houseless sons of chieftains,
　For their brethren near and far,
For the mourning Mother Island
　These their aspirations are.

And they say before up-rising:
　"Father! grant one other pray'r.
Bless the lord of Moy—O'Gara!
　Bless his lady and his heir!
Send the generous Chief, whose bounty
　Cheers, sustain us, in our task,
Health, success, renown, salvation:
　Father! grant the prayer we ask."

Oh, that we, who now inherit
　The great bequest of their toil,—
Were but fit to trace their footsteps
　Through the annals of the Isle;
Oh, that the same angel, Duty,
　Guardian of our tasks might be;
Teach us, as she taught our Masters,
　Faithful, grateful, just, to be :—
As she taught the old Four Masters
　In that Abbey by the sea !

THOMAS D'ARCY MCGEE.

THE DYING BARD.

Ask not a lay—my lyre is cold—
  My heart is chill'd, as by decay,
O'er-heaping it with funeral mould
  And muttering—"Clay, return to clay!"
So be it—let the happy shrink
  Aghast at time's unlook'd-for close—
I learnt from life, how calm can sink
  The wretched into death's repose.

Yet has my heart enough of life
  To blush for this intrusive strain;
For I had girt me for the strife
  Of soul with steel, of song with chain;
And though my place where none may grieve,
  Be measured,—yet it chafes my will
To perish from the earth, and leave
  My land beneath oppression still.

Yes!—mourn I must, to see the pall
  Drop o'er my visions unfulfill'd,
The last bright airy palace fall
  I pledged my very soul to build.
But one deep comfort still remains;—
  I am the humblest of the band
Who burned—and burn—to scorch the stains
  Of slavery from our fatherland.

The furnace will not miss one spark
 Evoked from its absorbing glow:
Strong men, by hosts, will strike our mark,
 Tho' lost be my light shaft and bow.
And so the meed be nobly won,
 Let glory shrine the conquering brave,
Tho' every pilgrim trample on
 My ashes in a neighbouring grave.

Oh, could I, ere my voice be hushed,
 See *all* unanimous as waves!—
No minstrel weeping, while he blushed,
 And sang upraiding songs—for slaves!
No chains, to make the heart a hell!
 No coward, to endure its fire!—
How gladly would I say: Farewell,
 My listener—and farewell, my lyre!

     J. De Jean Frazer.

NATIVE HILLS.

I KNOW, I know, each storied steep
    Thoughout the land,
Where winds—enchanted—love-locked sleep,
    Where teem the torrents grand,
For them I pine, for them I weep,
    An outcast man and banned.

I see the assembled bards of old
    On these grand hills;
Their music o'er the upland fold
    Like dew distils;
Or flashes downward bright and bold
    As cave-born rills.

Content thee, soul! in vain you long
    To breathe that air,
Sweet with the loving breath of song,
    Felt everywhere—
For man is weak, and Fate is strong:
    Not there! not there!

THOMAS D'ARCY MCGEE.

I LOVE YOU.

I LOVE you! 'tis the simplest way
  The thing I feel to tell;
Yet if I told it all the day,
  You'd never guess how well.
You are my comfort and my light,
  My very life you seem;
I think of you all day—all night
  'Tis but of you I dream.

There's rapture in the lightest word
  That you can speak to me;
My soul is like Æolian chord,
  And vibrates under thee.
I never read the love-song yet
  So thrilling, fond, or true,
But in my own heart I have met
  Some kinder thought for you.

I bless the shadows on your face,
  The light upon your hair;
I'd like for hours to sit and trace
  The passing changes there;
I love to hear your voice's tone,
  Although you should not say
A single word to dream upon,
  When that has died away.

L

Oh, you are kindly as the beam
　That warms where'er it plays;
And you are gentle as a dream
　Of happy future days;
And you are strong to do the right,
　And swift the wrong to flee;
And if you were not half so bright
　You're all the world to me!

ELLEN MARY DOWNING.

HOME THOUGHTS.

IF Will had wings
　How fast I'd flee
To the home of my heart
　O'er the seething sea!
If Wishes were power,
　If Words were spells,
I'd be this hour
　Where my own love dwells.

My own love dwells
　In the storied land
Where the holy wells'
　Sleep in yellow sand,

And the emerald lustre
  Of Paradise beams
Over homes that cluster
  Round singing streams.

I, sighing, alas!
  Dwell here alone;
My youth is as grass
  On an unsunn'd stone;
Bright to the eye,
  But unfelt below;
As sunbeams that lie
  Over arctic snow;

My heart is a lamp
  That love must re-light,
Or the world's fire-damp
  Will quench it quite;
In the breast of my dear
  My life-tide springs—
Oh! I'd tarry none here
  If Will had wings.

If Will had wings
  How fast I'd flee
To the home of my heart
  O'er the seething sea!

If Wishes were power,
If Words were spells,
I'd be this hour
Where my own love dwells.

THOMAS D'ARCY MCGEE.

———

MAURYÈ NANGLE; OR, THE SEVEN SISTERS OF NAVAN.

A FRAGMENT (unpublished).

OH, there are sisters—sisters seven,
As bright as any stars in heaven;
Save one, they all were snowy white,
And she, like oriental night:
Yet she was like unto the rest,
Had all their softness in her breast,
Their lights and shadows in her face,
And in her figure all their grace;
The brightest she of all the seven,
Yet all were bright as stars in heaven.

They had true lovers, every one,
Except the fairest—she had none;
Or rather say that she returned
Their love to none who for her burned;
For Maurye's timid, Maurye's mild,
And on her spirit undefiled

St. Brigid's* nuns their thoughts have bent;
She flies her sister's merriment.
They say they'll marry, every one,
But Mauryè says she'll be a Nun.

"Oh, wait awhile," her father said,
"Sweet Mauryè, wait till I am dead."
The nuns for her more firmly sought
To wean her from each worldly thought.
"Oh, you were made for God, not man"—
'Twas thus their pious plea began;
For much these pale recluses feared
As her gay sisters' nuptials neared.
"Oh, wait awhile," the Baron said,
"Sweet Mauryè, wait till they are wed."

A novice now, sweet Mauryè dwells
Within dark Odder's sacred cells;
Yet on her sisters' wedding day
She joins the chivalric array.
The brides were sweeter than their flowers,
The bridegrooms came from haughty towers,
For Nangle's† daughters are beneath
No lordly hand in lordly Meath.
The novice heart of Mauryè swells:
"Oh, dark," she sighs, "are Odder's cells!"

---

* Of Odder—a nunnery dedicated to St. Bride (St. Brigide, *hibernice*) in the parish of Skreen, co. Meath, in the 12th century.
† The Nangles were Barons of the Navan and figured much in the history of the Pale.

Yet vainly, on that wedding day
Her sisters and their gay grooms pray—
She grieves to part with those so dear,
But she is filled with pious fear ;
While Tuite and Tyrrell urged in vain,
Her tears fell down like Munster rain—
Malone and Bellew, Taaffe and Dease,*
"Oh, cease," she says, "in pity cease,
Or I must leave your wedding gay,
In Odder's walls to fast and pray."

The marriage rites are bravely done ;
But what ails her, the novice Nun ?
Oh, never had she seen an eye
Look into hers so tenderly !
"Methinks that deep and mellow voice
Would make the abbess' self rejoice ;
He's sure the saint I dreamt upon—
Not Barneville of Trimleston ;
In Holy Land his spurs he won—
What aileth me, a novice Nun ?"

.   .   .   .

Cetera desunt

* 'Tis clear the Nangles knew their rank, for these names were
among the best in Meath [Author's note].

THOMAS DAVIS.

MUSINGS AT SEA.

[Written to commemorate the first anniversary of Thomas
Davis's death.]

ALONE and pacing to and fro,
Or peering on the wave below,
Rise fast within me, as I muse,
Regrets, resolves, and sad adieus.

It hath a solemn charm to me
This nightfall on the tranquil sea,
With strangely mingled light and sound,
And Nature's mystic deeps around.

Their ceaseless plash the paddles make,
Phosphoric sparkles crest their wake—
The cluster'd lamps fade off on shore
And I need strain my eyes no more.

No cloud, save floating smoke and steam
Twin spirits, black and white, they seem.
The dusky chimney, mast and spars
Rise, ghostlike to the placid stars.

God's placid stars shine over all—
Their semblance meteors flash and fall;
So reign the blest in star-like peace—
So earthly glories gleam and cease.

Beside me frequent laughter rings,
With common talk of common things;
And evermore the thought is near
How mortal life is imaged here.

Thus buoyed upon a thin frail stay
That breaks around us day by day—
The dreaded gulf of gulfs below,
All thoughtless and secure we go.

And thus 'from dark to dark we sail
Our ken a dim and narrow pale—
Yet Heaven's true light is not denied,
And in us reigns a power to guide.

And thus—but let me cease a strain
For ever preached, and preached in vain;
I've crossed these waves with other tone,
Not moralizing nor alone.

With buoyant hope—with laughter free,
With hearts on fire for days to be,
With blood too boyish-bold that ran,
But all the thoughts and aims of man.

For Freedom then—not coy to win—
Seemed nigh our longing arms within:
Wide earth possess'd no other thing
Could claim such fervent worshipping.

We saw her form—it hovered o'er
Where kindling myriads met and swore;
We heard her in their pealing cheer—
Oh, what a future brighten'd near!

Beyond what flushing France had seen
When first she sprang a chainless Queen—
Her tameless might, her glorious gains
Untouched by guilt or impious stains.

A time of fiery act and word,
Of souls like mighty waters stirred,
Of sweeping thought, of loftiest will,
And sacrifices grander still.

Until from out that plastic glow
New forms of peaceful strength should flow,
And fair content and calm renown
Should gem transfigur'd Ireland's crown.

Oh, many a vaunt since then is stilled
And many a dear dream unfulfilled;
And one best hope of coming years
Lies quenched in grief and bitter tears.

Death's awful shadow passed between,
To teach what mortal visions mean—
Our noblest friend, our truest aid,
Cold in his vault we saw him laid.

Quenched is that glorious beacon—snapped
The bond so close around us wrapped;
Yet now before my dreaming eye
His image stands—how vividly!

I see that start of glad surprise—
The lip compressed, the moistened eyes;
I hear his deep impressive tone,
And feel his clasp, a brother's own.

Affections like a girl's were there,
With strength for all the strong could dare,
And fire whence flagging spirits drew
Fresh heat to rise and strive anew.

One aim was his that never stooped,
One idol-hope that never drooped;
One task to shatter Ireland's thrall,—
'Twas love, devotion—all-in-all.

Its greatness o'er his soul took hold,
And formed and fired to hero-mould—
Its beauty sank his bosom through
Until impassioned Song it grew!

Beloved and honoured!—with a sphere
Of proud exertion widening near,
In manhood's power and might arrayed—
Cold in the grave we saw him laid.

Not dying as he yearned to die,
Keened by his Country's victor-cry,—
But struck by swift and stern disease :—
How strange to man are God's decrees!

Well each, like him, must tread his way,
And hope and labour as he may ;
And each at last must meet his fate,
Too soon—or haply, far too late.

For me, thrice welcome Schiller's friend—
" Calm occupation : "—let me bend
To do the work that nearest lies,
And watch for other tasks to rise.

JOHN O'HAGAN.

EVENING THOUGHTS IN EXILE.

'TIS night in Ireland now, and those we love
Are dreaming of the distant and the dear ;
The stars upon the sea think of the stars above,
And fairy music mocks the sleeper's ear.

Darkness is round the home I left behind,
　Silence along the old familiar way;
The unshut gate swings sadly in the wind,
　The ivy o'er the wall has gone astray.

　　Oh, my home, my lost home, my loved home!
　　　There can never be another home for me—
　　My soul flies nightly back through the wild winds
　　　　and foam,
　　　And with its wet wings hovereth over thee.

Here, the gorgeous sunset scenes tires my eyes,
　A lovely and a liberal land is here!
But gladly would I part from it to-morrow, and arise
　To return to you, my unforgotten dear!

For your hills surround my heart like a wall,
　And your paths are all winding through my brain,
And in my ears there echoeth the deep foamy fall,—
　Shall I never sit within its spray again?

　　Oh, my home! my loved home! my lost home!
　　　How I long in thy close embrace to be!
　　But whereso'er I dwell, to whatever land I roam,
　　　I can never more be happy but with thee.

　　　　　　　THOMAS D'ARCY McGEE.

AMERICA'S INVITATION.

FRIENDS to Freedom! is't not time
  That your course were shaped at length?
  Wherefore stand ye loitering here?
Seek some healthier, holier clime,
  Where your souls may grow in strength,
  And whence Love hath exiled Fear!

Cross with me the Atlantic's foam,
  And your genuine goal is won.
  Purely Freedom's breezes blow,
Merrily Freedom's children roam
  By the dœdal Amazon,
  And the glorious Ohio!

Come!—if Liberty's true fires
  Burn within your bosoms, come!
  If ye would that in your graves
Your free sons would bless their sires,
  Make the Far Green West your home—
  Cross with us the Atlantic's waves!

JAMES CLARENCE MANGAN.

VERSICLES.

THE BANNER.

LITTLE I know what hero hand
   First flung a Banner on the air,
And gave to every eye that scanned
   The legend of its purpose there;
But well I know it was a deed
   Of right heroic pious strain,
To lift the spell-word of your creed
   Above the slaying and the slain—
   Above the purple battle rain—
Above the tumult-covered sod—
And fly it, silent, in the face of God!

DUTY.

WHEN God had made the world—while man
   Rose pliant 'neath His will,
And his lone eyes awoke to scan
   The world God's wonders fill;—
As, half inform—soft, plastic, warm,—
   Arose the nascent thought,
The Godhead wrote there one bright word,
   "The grand word, Ought,"*
And man looked up and blessed the Lord:
   And soul was wrought!

MARTIN MACDERMOTT.

* Emerson.

O! THAT MY VOICE COULD WAKEN.

(FROM THE IRISH.)

OH, that my voice could waken the hearts that
    slumber cold!
The chiefs that time hath taken, the warrior kings
    of old!
O! for Fingal, the pride of all the gallant Finnian crew
To wave his hand, the fight demand, and blow
    the *bar-abú!*

O! for the Clan-na-Morin, the Clan-na-Deaghaïd tall,
Dalriada's knights of glory, who scaled the Roman
    wall!
O! for the darts that smote the hearts of freedom's
    foreign foe,
When bloodier grew the fierce *Crobh-ruadh*, o'er
    bleak Helvetia's snow!

The fishers of Kilkernan, the men of Greenore bay,
The dwellers by Loch Dergert, and by the broad
    Loch Neagh,
Leave boat and oar, and leap ashore, to join the
    fiery ranks
Who come in pride from Gailtee's side, and from
    Blackwater's banks.

Where stubborn Newre is streaming—where Lee's
  green valley smiles—
Where kingly Shannon circles his hundred sainted
  isles—
They list the call, and woe befall the hapless doomed
  array
Who'll rouse their wrath on war's red path, to
  strike in freedom's fray.

I see the brave rejoicing—I hear their shouts ascend
See martyred men, approving, from thrones of
  brightness bend.
Ye ache my sight, ye visions bright, of all our glory
  won—
The " Battle's Eye * " hath found reply—my tuneful
  task is done !

EDWARD WALSH.

* " Battle's Eye "—Rosg-Catha : the war-song of the clan.

SALUTATION TO THE KELTS.

HAIL to our Keltic brethren wherever they may be,
In the far woods of Oregon, or o'er the Atlantic sea ;
Whether they guard the banner of St. George, in
　　Indian vales,
Or spread beneath the nightless North experimental
　　sails—
　　　　　　One in name, and in fame,
　　　　　　Are the sea-divided Gaels.

Though fallen the state of Erin, and changed the
　　Scottish land,
Though small the power of Mona, though
　　unwaked Lewellyn's band,
Though Ambrose Merlin's prophecies are held as idle
　　tales,
Though Iona's ruined cloisters are swept by northern
　　gales :
　　　　　　One in name, and in fame,
　　　　　　Are the sea-divided Gaels.

In Northern Spain and Italy our brethren also dwell,
And brave are the traditions of their fathers that
　　they tell :

The Eagle or the Crescent in the dawn of history pales
Before the advancing banners of the great Rome
conquering Gaels.*
> One in name, and in fame,
> Are the sea-divided Gaels.

A greeting and a promise unto them all we send ;
Their character our charter is, their glory is our end—
Their friend shall be our friend, our foe whoe'er
assails
The glory or the story of the sea-divided Gaels.
> One in name, and in fame,
> Are the sea-divided Gaels.

THOMAS D'ARCY MCGEE.
BOSTON, *August* 30th, 1850.

* The province of Gallicia in Spain (and the poet might have
added that of the same name in Poland, as well as the ancient Gal-
latia) are all of Gaelic origin. North Italy in Caesar's time, as we
all know, bore the name of Cisalpine *Gaul;* and Sienna, Sinigaglia
(Senogalliæ), as well as Sens in France, recall the presence of
the Gallic (or Gaelic) tribe of the Senones, whose Brenn (or
Brehon) captured Rome in the twilight of history. Not only
Ireland, but England, Scotland, France, Belgium, Switzerland
("Omnis Gallia" in fact) owe their earliest known inhabitants to the
race to which the Gael and Cymry belong ; and spoke the tongues,
one of which we *ought* to speak, and the other of which the
Welsh *do* speak. Anglo-Saxon, as the name of the English *race,*
is a misnomer : it ought to be *Kelto*-Saxon. The term Anglo-
Saxon is properly applicable to the language only, not to the
race.—ED,

PINING FOR THE DAWN.

THERE'S a motherland all beauty, sorrow-stricken,
    blind with tears,
Growing paler, growing weaker, with the heavy wrongs
    of years;
And her look of want and grief-tones pierce our
    bosoms, weak to save
The dear mother of our manhood from the name
    and doom of slave.
Oh, tis Eirè of the ocean !—Oh, tis Eirè of the
    song !
Oh, tis Eirè of lost glory !—she it is who drees
    this wrong.

" My sons," she says "are banished, or lie in lonely
    graves,
And the young and strong who're left me, flee for
    safety o'er the waves,
Scarce a voice is now uplifted ; scarce a hero-soul
    remains ;
While the stranger's pride grows bolder, as he smites
    me with his chains;"
In the night-time, in the day-time, still thy troubled
    voice I hear,
Injured mother ! all reproachful, hissing ever in my
    ear.

Oh, my brothers! we are guilty. We are obdurate
in hate.

We are the true enslavers!—we, the workers of
this fate!

Could we make a great forgiveness, brother taking
brother's hand,

Deathless honor should attend us as the saviours
of the land.

And the wan-look, and the grief-tones, and the
name and doom of shame

Would not torture, would not darken, mourning
Eirè's soul and fame.

Then, an island of all beauty, thronèd gladsome
on the sea,

Ruling wisely,—teaching widely,—would our rescued
Eirè be ;

And the deep ships of the nations, swarming
countless o'er the brine,

Swift would seek our desert havens with the spoils
of loom and mine,

Then again we'd greet our brothers whom the
stranger bore away—

Mother Eirè, we are pining for the Dawning of
the Day !

MAURICE RICHARD LEYNE.

THE DEAD ANTIQUARY O'DONOVAN.

FAR are the Gaelic tribes and wide
Scattered round earth on every side,
  For good or ill ;
They aim at all things, rise or fall,
Succeed or perish :—but, through all,
  Love Erin still.

Although a righteous Heaven decrees*
Twixt us and Erin stormy seas
  And barriers strong—
Of care, and circumstance, and cost—
Yet count not all your absent lost,
  Oh, Land of Song !

Above *your* roofs no star can rise
That does not lighten in *our* eyes ;
  Nor any set,
That ever shed a cheering beam
On Irish hillside, street or stream,
  That we forget.

And thus it comes that even I,
Though weakly and unworthily,
  Am moved by grief
To join the melancholy throng
And chant the sad entombing song
  Above the Chief :—

* These lines were written in America.

I would not do the dead a wrong:
If graves could yield a growth of song
        Like flowers of May,
Then Mangan from the tomb might raise
One of his old resurgent lays,—
        But, well-a-day!

He, close beside his early friend,
By the stark shepherd safely penned,
        Sleeps out the night;
So his weird numbers never more
The sorrow of the isle shall pour,
        In tones of might.

Though haply still, by Liffey's tide,
That mighty master must abide,
        Who voiced our grief
O'er Davis lost *; and he who gave
His free frank tribute to the grave
        Of Erie's Chief; †

Yet must it not be said that we
Failed in the rites of minstrelsy,
        So dear to souls
Like his whom lately death had ta'en
Altho' the vast Atlantic main
        Between us rolls!

* Samuel Ferguson.

† Denis Florence MacCarthy whose poem on the death of
O'Connell was one of the noblest tributes paid to the memory
of the great Tribune.—Author's Note. I need not add that
all the poets named—praising and praised—have since passed
away.—Ed.

Too few, too few, among our great,
In camp or cloister, church or state,
  Wrought, as he wrought;
Too few, of all the brave we trace
Among the champions of our race,
  Gave us his thought.

He toiled to make our story stand,
As from Time's reverent, runic hand
  It came, undecked
By fancies false; erect, alone,
The monumental arctic stone
  Of ages wrecked.

Truth was his solitary test,
His star, his chart, his east, his west;
  Nor is there aught
In text, in ocean, or in mine,
Of greater worth, or more divine
  Than this he sought.

With gentle hand he rectified
The errors of old bardic pride,
  And set aright
The story of our devious past.
And left it, as it now must last,
  Full in the light.

    THOMAS D'ARCY McGEE.

NOT FOR ME.

CARELESS of the dark Hereafter
Fairy childhood's magic laughter
Lightly rings from floor to rafter,—
   Not for me.
Sunset's angel fondly hovers
O'er the sheltering copse that covers
All the world to whispering lovers—
   Not for me ! Not for me !

Love—the heart's immortal story !
Young, though Earth and Time be hoary,
Burns—shall burn—in fervid glory—
   But not for me.
Passion's tide hath ebbed for ever—
Dearest friendships wane and sever—
Murdered Love reviveth never,
   Never ! never ! more for me.

Not for me, in sylvan alleys,
Leafy nooks and happy valleys,
Loveliness confiding dallies,
   Woe is me !
Last farewells are writ and spoken
Sooner were the dead awoken,
Than renewed the jewel broken,
   Woe is me ! Woe is me !

Soon shall thrill the love-bird's measure,—
Spring unfold her living treasure,
Nature's smile in vernal pleasure,—
   Not for me.
Shadows veil the moon's reflection,
Blushes rise without detection,
Whispers thrill with pure affection,
   Not for me. Not for me.

Irish harps no more shall fire me,
Irish Beauty's lips inspire me—
Mute I mourn tho' joy desire me
   Woe is me!
Once the song not thus was wasted,
Beauty's burning lips untasted—
Ah, how swiftly summer hasted!
   Woe is me. Woe is me.

RICHARD D'ALTON WILLIAMS

AM I REMEMBERED IN ERIN?

Am I remember'd in Erin?
   I charge you, speak me true!
Has my name a sound—a meaning,
   In the scenes my boyhood knew?
Does the heart of the Mother ever
   Recall her exile's name?
For to be forgot in Erin,
   And on earth, were all the same.

Oh, Mother! Mother Erin!
   Many sons your age hath seen—
Many gifted constant lovers
   Since your mantle first was green;
Then how may I hope to cherish
   The dream that I could be
In your crowded memory number'd
   With that palm-crown'd company?

Yet faint and far, my Mother!
   As the hope shines on my sight.
I cannot choose but watch it
   Till my eyes have lost their light;
For never among your brightest
   And never among your best,
Was heart more true to Erin
   Than beats within my breast.

THOMAS D'ARCY McGEE.

A PRAYER TO ST. PATRICK.

SAINTED Apostle, guardian, guide and father!
    Throned with the blest on high,
Hear how the groans of age-long anguish gather—
    List to thy people's cry!
Remember when thy torch of faith was lighted
    Of old in Erin's Isle,
How, one and all, her fervent sons united
    To hail its radiant smile :—
But frantic discord since hath rent asunder
    Our state, and cause, and grace;
Till nations gaze in sorrow, scorn and wonder
    Upon our scattered race

Oh, blessèd Patrick! lowly now imploring
    We crave thy mighty aid,
While God's high justice humbly still adoring,
    Pray that this plague be stayed!
Pray that the centuries of our desolation
    Blotting the book of Time,
May have filled up the meed of expiation
    For our ancestral crime.
Pray that the seven-fold gift of God—the spirit
    Of wisdom, strength and love,
May heal our feuds and set us free to merit
    The brighter home above.

MRS. HOPE CONNOLLY.*

* "Thomasine" of the *Nation*.

EUGENE O'CURRY.

Give me again my harp of yew,
　In consecrated soil 'twas grown ;
Shut out the day-star from my view,
　And leave me with the night alone.
The children of this modern land*
　May deem our ancient custom vain,
But aye responsive to my hand,
　The harp must pour the funeral strain.

It was of old a sacred rite,
　A debt of honor freely paid,
To champions fallen in the fight,
　And scholars known in peaceful shade.
Alas ! that it should now be claimed,
　O World ! for one we least can spare ;
Whose name by us was never named
　Without its meed of praise and prayer.

An *Ollave* of the elect of old,
　Whose chairs were placed beside the king ;
Whose herds, whose hounds, whose gifts of gold,
　The later bards regretful sing.
Ay ! there was music in his speech
　And in his wand the power to save,
This sole Recorder—on the beach—
　Of all we've lost beneath the wave.

* Written in America.

Who are his mourners? by the hearth
　　His presence kindled, sad they sit;
They dwell throughout the living earth
　　In homes his presence never lit;
Where'er a Gaelic brother dwells,
　　There heaven has heard for him a prayer;
Where'er an Irish maiden tells
　　Her votive beads, his soul has share.

Where, far or near, or west or east,
　　Glistens the *sogarth's* sacred stole,
There from the true unprompted priest
　　Shall rise a *requiem* for his soul;
Such orisons like clouds shall rise
　　From every realm beneath the sun,
For where be now the shores or skies
　　The Irish *sogarth* has not won?

Oh! mortal tears will dry like rain,
　　And mortal sighs pass like the breeze,
And earthly prayers are oft in vain,
　　E'en breathed amid the Mysteries;
Happy alone we hold the man
　　Whose steps so righteously were trod;
Who 'ere the judgment act began,
　　Had supplicants in the Saints of God.

Arise ye cloud-borne saints of old,
    In number like the polar flock!
Arise, ye just, whose tale is told
    On Shannon's side and Arran's rock!
In number, like the waves of seas—
    In glory like the stars of night—
Arise, ambrosial-laden bees
    That banquet thro' heaven's fields of light!

This mortal, called to join your choir,
    Through every care and every grief,
Sought with an antique soul of fire
    O'er all, God's glory—first and chief:
And next he sought, oh, sacred band!
    Ye disinherited of heaven!
To give you back your native land—
    To give it as it first was given.

No more the widowed glen repines,
    No more the ruined cloister groans;
Back on the tides have come the shrines;
    Lo! we have heard the speech of stones!
In the mid-watch, when darkness reigned
    And sleepers slept, unseen his toil—
But heaven kept count of all he gained
    For ye, men of the Holy Isle!

THOMAS D'ARCY McGEE

A VERY OLD, OLD, MAN.

"I MUST be very old," I keep
  Repeating o'er and o'er ;
And yet, by the old bible-page
(Where our good father marked my age)
  My years are twenty-four.
What, twenty-four! Life's sunny prime!
  Life's early Age of Gold !
When thought is warm, when hopes are bright,
And hearts still bathed in young delight—
  Ah, no ! *my* heart is cold,
  I must be very, very old—
   A very Old, Old, Man !

They say, my hairs are thick and brown—
  I *feel* them thin and gray ;
They say, my cheek—though pale—still bears
No furrowed trace of tears or cares—
  I care not what they say.
Does my step totter? No, I pace
  Erect and firm, and bold !
What then?—Deep underneath the lid
Of my strong heart, the worm is hid—
  The worm that's keen and cold :
  Ah, me ! I must be very old—
   A very Old, Old, Man.

For why? The glad sun's genial rays
    Fail to make my heart glad;
And strangely as a thing foregone
Striketh youth's soaring, joyous tone
    Upon my soul so sad.
I love the night time more than day—
    The night, with stars so cold;
And better quiet thought than mirth,
Though it were round a Christmas hearth
    Where tales of love are told.
    In sooth I must be very old—
        A very Old, Old, Man.

I know not now (I am so old)
    How long it is ago:
But, sure, it must be very long!
Since I beheld a Nation, strong
    In hope and valour grow;
Her voice was loud, her bearing proud,
    And glorious to behold!
And now where is she? What is she?
A beggar upon bended knee,
    A slave that's bought and sold:
    Indeed, I must be very old—
        A very Old, Old, Man.

Besides, doth not the good God give
    Life, its appointed span—
Some more, some less, but still enow
To let sweet flowers and green grass grow
    Upon the grave of man?

But I have seen Death strike so fast
    That church-yards could not hold,
Though torn into one general grave,
The remnants of the young, the brave,
    The bright-eyed and the bold !
    I must be very, very old—
      A very Old, Old, Man.

Or say, I am not old, or say,
    My years are twenty-four :
Alas ! when sorrows come so fast,
So thickly crowd so short a past,
    What boot years less or more ?
While in my heart I feel the change,
    In sorrows manifold :
When bright hopes wane, like summer-eves,
And human creatures fall, like leaves
    Upon the autumn mould—
    I know, I feel, I *must* be old—
      A VERY Old, Old, Man.

                MARTIN MacDERMOTT.

SIR BANNERET OF THE TRICOLOR.

WHET my sabre, my cuirass bind,·
Sling my carabine far behind ;
Loose my bannerol broad and free,
For I am a knight of high degree—
Of a famous Order, whose lists were old
When Charlemagne blazoned the Book of Gold ;
Whose Free Companions had won renown,
Ere Brutus stabbed the Cæsar down.
   A Banneret of the Tricolor !
   Banneret knight of the Tricolor !
   Ladies' graces and trophies *go leor*
   To the Banneret of the Tricolor !

Not mine to be dubbed by a royal blade,
Nor won my spurs by a noble's raid—
Oh ! I knelt for the knightly accolade
At the back of a Paris barricade ;
I kept the vigil our laws ordain
While the bombs fell fast around the Madeleine,
And swore my vow at Ventura's knee
To fight to the death for Liberty !
   Life and death for the Tricolor !
   Banneret true of the Tricolor !
   Freedom's vassal for evermore
   Is the Banneret of the Tricolor !

In Berlin streets there are broad platoons,
Down Berlin streets ride the fierce dragoons,
In Berlin streets there are dripping blades,
And the cry is, "Up with the barricades!'"
Who heads the charge through the Konig-
    strasse,
Who points the grape where the Yagers pass,
Whose gallop splashes the gutters of gore?
'Tis the Banneret of the Tricolor!
          The Eagle under the Tricolor!
          Black and Red on the Tricolor!
          Through showers of bullets and streams
              of gore,
          Rides the Banneret of the Tricolor!

The day that I sat by Guyon's side!—
After the Bann, the Serezans ride,
And many a league we could track their trail
By smoking roof-tree and woman's wail—
Christ! how we galloped their lances down
And battered their files in Mannswerth town,
Till the Austrian bugles brayed retreat;
As I clove a Croat from crown to seat.
          Charging for Hungary's Tricolor,
          The ancient Magyar Tricolor,
          'Twill wave from the walls of Pesth
              once more;
          God guard Kossuth and the Tricolor!

Dear Di Lana! a day will be
For Freedom's smile over Sicily;
And from Etna's top to Messina's shore
The tyrant's frown shall be death no more.
We'll fling old Bomba the crater down;
Thy statue 'll stand in Palermo town,
As when you sprung forth, sword in hand,
Like Joan of Arc, for native land.

> Oh, Ensign fair of the Tricolor,
> The lilies yield to the Tricolor,
> We'll trample their bloom on the golden
> shore,
> And raise the glorious Tricolor.

And thou, old natal Isle! again
I hear the tramp of thine armed men;
And aye once more the day shall come
For the bristling steel and rolling drum!
I see through the battle's lurid haze,
The Orange and Green on thy banner blaze,
And the Blue gleam high over files of steel
Where the tyrant's squadroons backward reel!

> On with the glorious Tricolor!
> Fight to the death for the Tricolor!
> Shroud in death and pennon before
> Sir Banneret of the Tricolor!

J. CASHEL HOEY.

24th May, 1851.

THE GREEN FLAG.

AIR—" *The Wearing of the Green.*"

THE Green Flag—the Green Flag! oh, would that
    it flew
As proudly in the Old Land as 'tis flying in the
    New!
The West and South gave honoured place unto its
    radiant sheen,
And our Exiles build their homes beneath the
    banner of the Green.

> Oh the South loves the Green, for the
>   summer's shining there,
> While here the winter, dim and cold, is
>   bleak as our despair;
> And the numbing snow-drifts cover every
>   path where once was seen
> The pride and promise of the spring—the
>   glory of the Green.

Once gallant hands upheld the flag, and hearts
    were throbbing high
With fiery love that deemed it joy for that dear
    cause to die.
Now strangers mock its drooping folds, and scoffing
    pass it by,
While round it swells no battle song, but slavery's
    feeble sigh.

> Oh, the South loves the Green, &c.

Alas, alas .for Eirè ! ah, the friends are faint and
few
That still guard round the emblem of her spirit
bright and true ;
Yet day by day some shrink away, or turn their
hearts and eyes
To where the Green is waving free beneath the
Southern skies.

But sure as God renews again the glory of
the year,
Our Winter yet shall pass away—the Summer
shall be here ;
Beneath the snow revives the glow in Ireland's
breast, I ween,
And faithful lovers yet shall twine fresh garlands of the Green.

MRS. HOPE CONNOLLY.

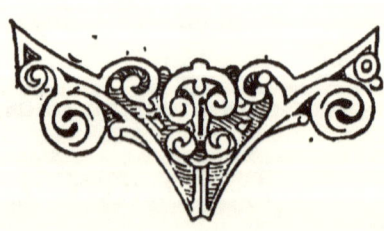

OUR PARLIAMENT—A STREET BALLAD.

AIR—"*Fagh an Bealach.*"

[The following note is appended to this ballad in the copy of it first printed in the "Memoir of Thomas Davis" by Sir Charles Gavan Duffy :—"Here is a street ballad, written with something of the plainness and vigour of Swift, which he (Davis) probably intended for an experiment often debated, and made by some of his friends after his death, of substituting sense and spirit for the incoherent nonsense which made up the bulk of ballads sung to the people."]

'Twas once in College Green, boys,
　Our Parliament, our Parliament,
But its blessings might be seen, boys,
　Where'er you went, where'er you went.
'Twas won by armèd men, boys,
　The Volunteers, the Volunteers ;
We were united then, boys,
　And had no fears, and had no fears.

The arms that won our right, boys,
　Were crossed in wrath, were crossed in wrath ;
But England urged the fight, boys,
　To weaken both, to weaken both ;
And some were English slaves, boys,
　Who bent, alas ! who bent, alas !
And some were greedy knaves, boys,
　Who sold the pass, who sold the pass.

And thus they took away, boys,
  Our Parliament, our Parliament.
Our curse upon the day, boys,
  When off it went, when off it went.

But as our fathers did, boys,
  In Eighty-two, in Eighty-two,
And right and honour bid, boys,
  Their sons can do, their sons can do.
Let Protestant unite, boys,
  With Catholic, with Catholic,
And we'd, this very night, boys,
  The English lick, the English lick.
'Twas once in College Green, boys,
  Our Parliament, our Parliament,
And there it shall be seen, boys,
  Or they'll repent, they'll repent.

THOMAS DAVIS.

PAT AS A LANDLORD.

I HAVE a farm of my own,
  I pay rent to nobody;
Crouching and whining are gone,
  I'm the tenant of nobody!
Now I have courage to toil,
  Since what I earn is sure to me;
I can work like a slave of the soil,
  For all that it yields is secure to me.
    Chorus (digs) "I have a farm of my own," &c.

I have a mind of my own,
  I'll be fooled by nobody;
I can act, or let it alone,
  Driven or hinder'd by nobody.
The farmer, of old, was no man,
  Many's the time I lamented it;
Now, we've a serf-freeing plan,
  My blessings on those who invented it!
    Chorus (digs) "I have a farm of my own," &c.

All that I have is my own,
  I owe duty to nobody;
I can labour, or let it alone,
  I give my work to nobody.

I have no agent to tease—
I have no bailiff to bother me;
I'll vote for whoever I please
However they try to *soother* me.
Chorus (*digs*) " I have a farm of my own," &c.

THOMAS D'ARCY McGEE.

THE IRISH RAPPAREES.

A PEASANT BALLAD.

[When Limerick was surrendered and the bulk of the Irish army took service with Louis XIV., a multitude of the old soldiers of the Boyne, Aughrim and Limerick preferred remaining in the country at the risk of fighting for their daily bread ; and with them some gentlemen, loath to part from their estates or their sweethearts. The English army and the English law drove them by degrees to the hills, where they were long a terror to the new and old settlers from England, and a secret pride and comfort to th trampled peasantry, who loved them even for their excesses. It was all they had left to take pride in.]

RIGH SHEMUS he has gone to France and left his
    crown behind :—
Ill-luck be theirs, both day and night, put runnin'
    in his mind !

Lord Lucan* followed after, with his slashers brave
    and true,
And now, the doleful *keen* is raised—" What will
    poor Ireland do ?
        " What must poor Ireland do ?
" Our luck, they say, has gone to France. What
    can poor Ireland do ?"

Oh, never fear for Ireland, for she has so'gers still,
For Remy's boys are in the wood, and Rory's on
    the hill ;
And never had poor Ireland more loyal hearts
    than these—
May God be kind and good to them, the faithful
    Rapparees !
        The fearless Rapparees !
The jewel waar ye, Rory, with your Irish Rappa-
    rees !

Oh, black's your heart, Clan Oliver, and coulder
    than the clay !
Oh, high's your head, Clan Sassenach, since Sars-
    field's gone away !

---

* After the Treaty of Limerick. Patrick Sarsfield, Lord Lucan,
sailed with the Brigade to France, and was killed while leading
his countrymen to victory at the battle of Landen, in the Low
Countries, 29th July, 1693.

It's little love you bear to us for sake of long
    ago—
But howld your hand, for Ireland still can strike a
    deadly blow—
             Can strike a mortal blow
Och! *dar-a-Chreesth!* 'tis she that still could strike
    the deadly blow!

The Master's bawn, the Master's seat, a surly
    *bodach** fills;
The Master's son, an outlawed man, is riding on
    the hills;
But, God be praised, that round him throng, as
    thick as summer bees,
The swords that guarded Limerick walls—
    Rapparees!
             His lovin' Rapparees!
Who daar say *no* to Rory Oge, who heads the
    Rapparees!

Black Billy Grimes, of Latnamard, he racked us
    long and sore—
God rest the faithful hearts he broke, we'll never
    see them more!

---

* *Bodach:* a severe, inhospitable man.

But I'll go bail he'll break no more while Truagh
    has gallows-trees,
For why? he met one lonesome night the awful
    Rapparees!
           The angry Rapparees!
They never sin no more, my boys, who cross the
    Rapparees.

Now, Sassenach, and Cromweller, take heed of
    what I say—
Keep down your black and angry looks that scorn
    us night and day;
For there's a just and wrathful Judge that every
    action sees,
And He'll make strong, to right our wrong, the
    faithful Rapparees!
           The fearless Rapparees!
The men that rode at Sarsfield's side, the changeless
    Rapparees!

CHARLES GAVAN DUFFY.

1850.

THE LAST OF OUR BAND.

LOST are the brave and true, Erin!
They fell from me and you, Erin!
   But though my heart be chill,
   Stirred by no joyful thrill,
Oh! it is faithful still, Erin.

I loved you long ago, Erin!
I don't forget you now, Erin!
   But then, my heart was light,
   Planning your glory bright,
You make it sad to-night, Erin.

When will your tears be past, Erin?
When will you smile at last, Erin?
   Which of us all who make
   Struggle for your dear sake
Will see your fetters break, Erin?

From our ranks, day by day, Erin!
The faithfulest pass away, Erin!
   Oh, if but one remain, ·
   When thou has snapt thy chain—
Will he feel joy or pain, Erin?

Though he give back thy smile, Erin,
Must he not weep the while, Erin?
    Smile—to behold thee free,
    Weep—that *they* cannot see;
Sad will the triumph be, Erin.

ELLEN MARY DOWNING

APPENDIX.

◆

BIOGRAPHICAL NOTES.

◆

ANONYMOUS.

MRS. HOPE CONNOLLY.

THIS lady, who wrote for the *Nation* under the name of "THOMASINE," has lived for many years in or near Brisbane. A volume of her poems was recently published in this country, with an introduction by Sir Charles Gavan Duffy.

THOMAS DAVIS.

THE greatest of the patriot-poets of Ireland. Born at Mallow, Co. Cork, October 14th, 1814. B.A., T.C.D., 1836. Died, September 16th, 1845. Davis rightly signed his early contributions to the *Nation*, " A True Celt," his father, an eminent military surgeon, belonging to a family of Welsh extraction, settled in England— and his mother an O'Sullivan-Beare, thus combining in his person the two strains of pure Keltic blood. He became a barrister but never practised. After an exhaustive study of the historical records of Ireland, doing violence to his family tradition, he became an enthusiastic Nationalist, identifying himself wholly with the cause of the Gaelic majority of the Irish people, but always inculcating a cordial and fraternal fusion of races and creeds. When Sir Charles Gavan Duffy conceived the idea of founding the *Nation* newspaper, it was to Davis and his friend John Dillon that he applied for literary assistance in that undertaking. Thenceforward during the three years that remained of life, no man ever laboured so strenuously, or accomplished so much. The true value of his work for Ireland is only now becoming fully appreciated. The verses printed in this volume were all published after Davis's death. A small volume of Davis's poems, edited by his college friend, Thomas Wallis, was published in 1846, and has gone through many editions.

ELLEN MARY DOWNING.

BORN in Cork in 1828. Died, January 27th, 1869, at the Ursuline Convent of the same city. A sad and beautiful life history. Perhaps some day it may be given to the world.

CHARLES GAVAN DUFFY.

Now Sir Charles Gavan Duffy, K.C.M.G. Born in
Co. Monaghan in 1816. Received his education in
the town of the same name, from which, shortly after
leaving school, he came to Dublin where, as a lad, he
performed the duties of sub-editor in the office of *The
Morning Register*. Thence he removed to Belfast,
becoming editor first, and then proprietor of the
Belfast Vindicator. Here he married a grand-daughter
of the MacDermott of Coulavin, a charming lady who
survived but a short time the birth of a son, now the
Hon. John Gavan Duffy, who, following in his father's
footsteps, has held various ministries in the Victorian
legislature. Sir Gavan Duffy's work in the *Nation* and
the control he exercised for many years over Irish
politics in advancing the National cause are things
too well-known to require more than a reference to
them here. He wrote many great and vigorous
poems ; but this is not his greatest gift. It was not
poetry he brought to the party so much as the power
of initiation and organization, without which, notwith-
standing Davis's splendid talents there never would
have been a *Nation* newspaper, or a Young Ireland
party—any more than there would have been the old
Library of Ireland, or the new. Davis did splendid
work in the *Citizen*, and it fell dead ; splendid work in
the *Register*, in concert with John Dillon, and the
circulation fell off. His first success was in the

Nation, and it was attributable not only to his own splendid gifts, but to the method in which that journal was organized, launched and sustained. Of the work done by Duffy after the collapse in 1848, first in the English Parliament (work on which Parnell said before the Commission that he had modelled his own) and afterwards in the Parliament of Victoria where as Minister of Lands he devised and passed the greatest democratic measure of land distribution with which any State has ever been endowed—it would be irrelevant here to extend this reference. The "New Irish Library," as well as the old, has reason to be proud of its projector.

DE JEAN FRAZER.

BORN in King's County about 1809. Died March, 1852, in Dublin. A cabinet-maker by trade. Was a frequent contributor to the *Nation* from almost its earliest days. His poems are remarkable for their beautiful imagery, intense feeling, rush, and poetic sensibility. His life to its close appears to have been passed in ungenial surroundings, and in poverty. Of Northern extraction, and originally a Presbyterian, Frazer gave himself heart and soul to the National cause. A volume of Frazer's poems was published in Dublin, but it is probably out of print.

ARTHUR GERALD GEOGHEGAN.

BORN in Dublin, June 1st, 1810. Spent nearly 50 years of his life in the Excise, from which he retired as Collector of Inland Revenue in 1877. Died in London, where he had resided for a great number of years, November 12th, 1889. His best poem is the introduction to his " Monks of Kilcrea," but it does not belong to the *Nation* series, in which, however, he published a great many fine and stirring ballads. Sir C. G. Duffy in the "League of North and South," writing of the time (1855) when—relinquishing his long struggle against the forces of compression and corruption—he determined to carve out for himself a new career at the antipodes, mentions without naming them three friends who came forward with eager spontaneity to proffer him help. One of these he refers to thus :—" An Irishman, in the public service of England, whom I had never seen, and knew at the time only as a Protestant nationalist of remarkable literary gifts, *offered me the savings of his lifetime to be repaid at discretion.*" That Irishman I am authorised to say was Arthur Gerald Geoghegan.

Page
26   1. THE MOUNTAIN FERN.

———

JOHN CASHEL HOEY.

BORN in Dundalk, 1828; died in Kensington, January 6th, 1892. Became editor of the *Nation* when Duffy retired from that position in 1855. Afterwards for many years secretary at the Agency-General of Victoria, to which position he had been appointed by his former chief, when Prime Minister of that great colony. Hoey edited Lord Plunket's Speeches and otherwise contributed extensively to contemporaneous literature.

Page
168   1. SIR BANNERET OF THE TRICOLOR.

MAURICE RICHARD LEYNE.

BORN in Kerry, and was a grandson of O'Connell. In the contest between O'Connell and the Young Irelanders, he joined the latter, an heroic sacrifice considering the circumstances. He was of a most genial and loyal character, an effective speaker and writer, and a fellow of infinite humour, which he employed in lashing unsparingly the humbugs and traitors of "The Irish Brigade." The editor regrets that the brilliant pasquinades written by Leyne lie beyond the scope of this publication. He became a State prisoner in 1848, and joined the *Nation* after its revival in 1849. He died in 1855.

Page
153   1. PINING FOR THE DAWN.

JAMES McBURNEY ("CARROLL MALONE.")

SIR GAVAN DUFFY says, "all he knows about this admirable ballad-writer is that he was a County Down man; that he emigrated to the United States; and that he believes he died there only last year" (1892).

Page
80   1. THE GOOD SHIP CASTLE DOWN.

DENIS FLORENCE MacCARTHY.

BORN in Dublin in 1817 ; and died there on April 7th, 1882. A volume of his poems has been published, chiefly containing verses published in the *Nation*, but omitting many of the more National and all of the humourous from the collection. MacCarthy was more entirely the *homme-de-lettres* than any of his associates in the *Nation* circle. He translated a great quantity of Calderon's plays, wrote a Centenary Ode to Moore, etc., He was noted for the brilliancy of his wit, which flashed out into rapartee on the slightest provocation—at least that was his characteristic as a young man.

THOMAS D'ARCY McGEE.

BORN in Carlingford, Co. Louth, in 1825; died by assassination in Ottawa, Canada, on the night of April 7th, 1868. Went first to the United States in 1842, becoming editor of the *Boston Pilot* at the early age of 17. Returned to Ireland in 1844 and soon after joined the editorial staff of the *Nation*. He wrote some early books of much interest for the original *Library of Ireland*—one relating to Irish writers of the 17th century. Returning to America after the outbreak of 1848, he spent some years in travelling from place to place in the States—lecturing, editing Irish newspapers, and delivering pub ic addresses.   Eventually McGee settled in Canada where he almost immediately became a member of the legislature and one of the ministers of the Crown. His greatest work as a statesman was the leading part he took in the Federation of the Canadian States.   Indeed the foundation of the Dominion of Canada may be said almost to owe its inception and completion to Thomas D'Arcy McGee.   To weld half the American continent into one all but independent State, on the principle of automatic liberty for each of its territorial and racial divisions, was a work of superb achievement, reserved for few men.

The editor has elsewhere alluded to McGee's poems.

MARTIN MacDERMOTT.

BORN in Dublin in 1823 ; an architect by profession ; editor of the *New Spirit of the Nation.* Deputed to represent in Paris the political leaders of 1848. Served in Egypt for some years as Chief Architect to the Office of Works of the Khedive of Egypt.

JAMES CLARENCE MANGAN.

BORN in Dublin, May 1st, 1803. Died, June 20th, 1849. The editor has written at such length in the introduction of this gifted and unfortunate Irishman that nothing more need be said here. The best account of him is to be found in Fr. Charles P. Meehan's Introduction to the "Poets and Poetry of Munster," translated by J. C. M.   (Third Edition.)

Mrs. KEVIN O'DOHERTY.

THERE is a delightful legend attached to this lady
and her husband, Dr. Kevin Izod O'Doherty, who was
tried in 1848 for Treason-Felony along with his friend,
Richard D'Alton Williams. Williams had a friend in the
Crown Solicitor, who by a dexterous *tour-de-main* concealed the only paper incriminating him; but O'Doherty,
though having no friend in court, might have escaped,
had he been willing to plead guilty. He took counsel
with his fiancée—but she bravely said " No : don't.
I'll wait for you." She did, and they were married
the *day after he arrived* in Ireland, a free man.
" Eva " was this lady's name as a poetess, Eva Mary
Kelly her name as a heroine, and Mrs. Kevin Izod
O'Doherty that which she bears as a matron in Brisbane
where she has lived with her husband for many years.
Both were back in this country some little time ago,
but have now returned.

Page

68   1. Song of the Irish Minstrel.

JOHN O'HAGAN.

BORN at Newry, Co. Down, in 1822. Called to the
Irish bar in 1842; married the youngest daughter
of Lord O'Hagan in 1865; appointed judge of the
Irish Land Court in 1881, and died on November
12th, 1890. O'Hagan, though a much younger man,

had been a friend of Davis's in Trinity College; and when the *Nation* was started in 1842, he and his bosom-friend, John E. Pigot, became intimately connected with the working of it, forming with Duffy, Davis and Dillon, "the inner council of five," who met weekly to discuss nationality and literature. In 1848 O'Hagan took no active part except as junior counsel for the various political prisoners of that stirring era. In latter years he became a Justice of the Queen's Bench and head of the Irish Land Commission. He was a man of great intellectual balance and power, a most excellent and amiable man, and a fine poet :— *ecce signum.*

REV. J. F. TORMY, D.D.

BORN in Westmeath in 1820. Died in the same county in 1893. Father Tormy edited the *Tablet* with marked ability during Lucas's enforced absence in Rome. He spent many years in America.

Mrs. VARIAN.

THE pseudonym of this lady in the *Nation* was " FIONNUALA." She is still living, it is believed, in the County Cork.

EDWARD WALSH.

BORN in Londonderry in 1805. Died, August 6th, 1850. He appears to have led a wandering unstable life alternating between teaching and literature. The last we see of him is in a pathetic entry in Mitchel's " Jail Journal," where he just for a brief moment comes into the court-yard of the jail to whisper a word of sympathy with the prisoner, he being then the schoolmaster to the convicts. What a position for a man of real genuis—which Edward Walsh undoubtedly was.

LADY WILDE.

MAIDEN name, Jane Francesca Elgee, the widow of Sir W. R. Wilde, a distinguished surgeon, well-known for his devotion to Irish archæology and topographical studies.   The editor has spoken of Lady Wilde's great gift of song in his Introduction.   She lives in London and is the mother of Oscar and William Wilde.

RICHARD D'ALTON WILLIAMS.

BORN in Tipperary (or, as some say, in Dublin) in 1821. His father was Count D'Alton, a landed proprietor in Co. Tipperary—whose name, along with his mother's, he bore.   The secret of his parentage has never been made known, but one can see that it rankled in his heart all through his life who will read his last poem, " A Breeze Through the Forest."   He sent his first poem "The Munster War Song" from Carlow College while he was still a student there in 1843.   Williams had an abundant sense of humour ; and when, about 1844, he became a medical student in Dublin, he kept the readers of the *Nation* on a broad grin with the adventures of a certain member of his tribe whose merry pranks he translated into the Greek dialect of the dissecting room. But unfortunately these rhapsodies are not transplantable. How rare a quality is universal humour! Only once in centuries one meets with a Rabelais.—Williams like all humourists was also very melancholy. As his works have been published separately by a kindred poet, T. D. Sullivan, I forbear to make any long citations here.

[Note.—For many dates and particulars given in the foregoing *Notes*, the editor is indebted to the minute research of Mr. D. J. O'Donoghue in his Biographical Dictionary of Irish Poets.]